P9-CSS-442

People PROFILES

JOHN F. KENNEDY JR.
A BIOGRAPHY

BY J.D. REED,
KYLE SMITH &
JILL SMOLOWE

▪ CORRECTION ▪

A photo caption in our July issue identified the woman
with Tom and Jim Hanks and Rita Wilson as Jim Hanks's wife,
Karen Praxel. In fact, the woman is Lily Reeves, Rita Wilson's sister. In
another photo, the two actors with Tom Hanks were Johnathon Schaech
on the far left and Tom Everett Scott in the background.

■ TABLE OF CONTENTS ■

JOHN F. KENNEDY JR.

PIED PIPER

On September 7, 1995, in the rotunda of Manhattan's Federal Hall, where George Washington delivered the country's first inaugural address in 1789, John F. Kennedy, Jr. strode to a podium before an expectant audience of journalists, photographers and publishing colleagues. A vigorous 34-year-old, poured into a dark, European-style double-breasted suit, sporting a confident and slightly bemused smile, Kennedy simplifed matters by answering all questions about his personal life in one fell swoop, without anyone having to even raise a hand.

Looking down at his notes, he read, suave, straight-faced: "Yes. No. Honestly, we're just really good friends. None of your business. It's a possibility. Somewhere down the road maybe. She's my cousin from Rhode Island. Never in New Jersey."

And just that fast, as he had done countless times before,

"He was still becoming the person he would be," said Senator Edward Kennedy in his eulogy of John (four months before he died). "He had only just begun. There was in him a great promise of things to come."

Kennedy deftly defused the tension that always attended his arrival in a public place. Without revealing anything about those hobby-horses of press speculation—his political aspirations, his romantic life and his plans for the future—Kennedy focused attention on what he had come to announce. "Ladies and gentlemen," he said, "meet *George.*"

A black cloth was whisked away, revealing a larger-than-life-size cover of the first issue of *George*, the magazine he and the French publishing empire Hachette-Filipacchi would launch that month. On the cover: supermodel Cindy Crawford, campily costumed as George Washington, in powdered wig, black coat with brass buttons—and naughtily exposed navel. *George*, John said, would explore "the intersection of politics and popular culture."

Like few others, John F. Kennedy Jr. lived his entire life at that busy intersection, and made it seem a comfortable, even enviable, place. To reach that moment on the podium he had traced a path sometimes tragic, sometimes magical, always beguiling to the outside world. He was both a privileged prince and a loveable underdog. A gentleman, no scholar. An unusually likeable Lothario. In his tragically short lifetime JFK Jr. engendered affection rather than awe, acceptance rather than resentment. The public rooted for him, never more so than when he found a soul-mate in the elegant, entrancing Carolyn Bessette. They would spend a thousand days together as husband and wife—a numerically eerie echo of the thousand days his father spent in the White House.

▪ GROWING UP IN PUBLIC ▪

When John, Carolyn and her sister Lauren Bessette perished in the crash of his Piper Saratoga II in the ocean off Martha's Vineyard on July 16, 1999, he was just 38—eight years younger than his father, President John F. Kennedy, had been when he was assassinated in Dallas in 1963. "From the first day of his life," John's uncle, U.S. Senator Edward M. Kennedy, told some 300 mourners

not just
politics as
usual.

John Kennedy
talks to
George
Wallace

President
Madonna

Dodging
bullets
with
the FBI's
Louis
Freeh

Caleb Carr on
the next american

■ *"For me," Kennedy said at the September 1995 press conference
that launched his magazine* George, *"the marriage of publishing
and politics simply weaves together the two family businesses."*

at a private memorial service for John at the Church of St. Thomas
More in New York City on July 23, "John seemed to belong not
only to our family, but to the American family. The whole world
knew his name before he did."

Americans delighted to watch John Jr. romp in the Oval Office
while JFK looked on with joy. They clasped him permanently to
their hearts when, just a pudgy-kneed three-year-old in short
pants, he saluted the flag-draped casket of his slain father. That
correct, right-hand salute had melted, as TV cameras rolled, into a
child's unselfconscious gesture, the left hand lifting, two soft
uncertain fists rubbing eyes that had already seen too much.

Growing up in New York City (to which he would return as an
adult) John learned from his mother, Jacqueline Bouvier Kennedy
Onassis the virtues of self-reliance, kindness and grace under the

9

After the memorial at New York City's Church of St. Thomas More, Ted Kennedy and wife Victoria (second from right), talked with a priest. "You wonder how [they] endure the loss," says former RFK aide John Seigenthaler.

pressure of unflagging, unwanted attention. "Never let them steal your soul," Jackie famously advised John and his older sister, Caroline, about the ever-present paparazzi. He never did, exhibiting an ease before the cameras that his father, and his father's father, would have admired.

▪TREASURING HIS LEGACY▪

When he headed off to boarding school and then to Brown University, John learned more about what it meant to be a Kennedy. "He had a legacy, and he learned to treasure it," Ted Kennedy said during his eulogy. "He was part of a legend, and he learned to live with it."

That wasn't always easy. John abandoned his college passion for acting and plunged dutifully into law school—basic training for Kennedys. A career in politics beckoned; all he needed to do was toss his hat into the ring.

But which hat, and which ring? Perhaps an editor's eyeshade suited him best—not to mention a tasselled knit cap for boulevarding through nippy New York City winters. Kennedy abandoned the bar and founded *George*. He imbued the monthly with his own rakish energy, earnest curiosity and distrust of bombast. Despite numerous provocations—even from we at PEOPLE, who dubbed him The Sexiest Man Alive in 1988—he charmingly resisted the temptation to take himself too seriously. Kennedy played Frisbee in Central Park, baseball cap backwards. He biked to work at his magazine. He had one of the most recognizable, not to mention handsome, faces on earth, but he always cordially introduced himself to everyone he met.

Another temptation he resisted was trumpeting his own good works, which were more extensive than any but those closest to him knew. He served on the board of Harvard's Institute of Politics, part of the School of Government named after his father. He founded the Reaching Up program, to train caregivers for the mentally disabled. He worked with the Robin Hood Foundation, a group dedicated to helping New York City's underprivileged people.

"John was so much more than those long-ago images emblazoned in our minds." said Ted Kennedy at his nephew's memorial. "He was a boy who grew into a man with a zest for life and a love of adventure. He was a pied piper who brought us all along."

PRINCE OF CAMELOT

On November 25, 1960, President-elect John F. Kennedy, aboard his private plane, the *Caroline*, was winging from Washington, D.C. to Palm Beach, Florida, for a meeting with his father and mentor, Joseph P. Kennedy, the financier and Prohibition-era bootlegger who had become ambassador to Britain. Seventeen days earlier, JFK had narrowly defeated Republican candidate Richard M. Nixon, and was set to become, at age 43, the youngest elected chief executive in American history.

After the Caroline landed in Florida, the pilot received an emergency radio message: Jacqueline Kennedy had unexpectedly gone into labor some three weeks early. She was being rushed to Washington's Georgetown University Hospital.

JFK didn't wait for his plane to be refueled, but jumped aboard the faster press airliner that had followed him, and headed home. En route, he received another urgent message: Delivered by

"He used to give us chewing gum because my mother didn't like us to chew gum," John told Prime Time Live *in 1992. "So we'd go over to the Oval Office at night, and he'd feed us gum under the desk."*

Cesarean section, weighing 6 lbs, 3 oz, John Fitzgerald Kennedy Jr. had entered the world. As he would do throughout his father's Presidency, John Kennedy Jr. had delightfully disrupted business as usual.

Although he was an otherwise healthy boy, John Jr. suffered from a lung ailment and spent his first days in a hospital incubator. So he missed much of the hubbub in the Kennedy household at 3307 N Street NW in Washington's brick-and-ivy Georgetown section. The staff was preparing to move on January 20 from the Federal-era townhouse to 1600 Pennsylvania Avenue. John's three-year-old sister, Caroline, looked after by the family's diminutive, gray-haired British nanny, Maud Shaw, was also packing. Dignitaries and politicians shuffled in and out on an almost hourly basis, meeting and consulting with JFK, who was busy staffing his administration. Outside, a small (by today's standards) corps of reporters and photographers huddled and hoped for tidbits.

▪ BABY YOU'RE A STAR ▪

The sense of great expectations was par for the course in this high-profile family. John and Jackie Kennedy were a glamorous couple, trailed by an adoring press long before John Jr. toddled onto the stage. Jack Kennedy had made his mark first as a war hero—rescuing injured crewmates after his famous torpedo boat, PT 109, was rammed and split in two by a Japanese destroyer—then as a U.S. Congressman and later as Senator from Massachusetts. JFK and Jackie—who preferred to be called "Jacleen"—were as near to a royal couple as a democracy could have. From the time of their 1953 marriage, the Kennedys lived—Jack more comfortably, and with more calculation, than his wife—in a halo of flashbulbs.

So it was no wonder that John's birth became a national news event: His feedings of Similac through the night, his ounce-by-ounce weight gain, were all duly reported. Recalls author William Manchester, who has written three books on JFK, including *The*

▧ *"Jackie [in 1962] worried more about John than about Caroline, who matured quickly and was very influenced by her father," says Jackie's step-brother Hugh Auchincloss Jr.. "Jackie paid special attention to John."*

Death Of A President, John "was famous for having been a child." Indeed, he became the most notable baby in America. Newspapers ran headlines such as "Jack Jr. To Leave Incubator Today" and "John-John Loses Tooth."

The personal and the political swirled together to create a new kind of pop saga. As John was being christened in Georgetown Hospital's small chapel, according to biographer Wendy Leigh's *Prince Charming*, JFK and his brother Robert Kennedy, who would serve the new administration as Attorney General, had a whispered argument in the pews about the new cabinet. The President-elect wanted the distinguished Arkansas Senator William Fulbright for his Secretary of State; Bobby was against it because he felt Fulbright was too conservative on social issues such as civil rights.

"When I arrived at Georgetown Hospital, the atmosphere was buoyant and joyous, almost carnival-like," recalls then-LIFE (and

15

"This was a remarkably 'normal' family," says veteran TIME columnist Hugh Sidey of the wealthy Kennedys (in Hyannis Port in 1962). "The playing field wasn't the same one [as ours]. Yet there was a normalcy about it."

later PEOPLE) correspondent Gail Wescott. "Security was minimal and President-elect Kennedy would wave from his wife's hospital room and then stop and talk with us all when he came downstairs. Back on N Street, we took marvelous pictures of him wheeling

Caroline in her stroller. It was innocent and exhilarating. It did not seem that anything could ever go wrong."

▪A STAR-CROSSED CLAN▪

John's parents knew better. They came to the White House from two branches of the American plutocracy, each with a history of accomplishment, wealth, passion and heartbreak. The Kennedy clan, of Brookline and Hyannis Port, Massachusetts, revolved around JFK's father, Joseph P. Kennedy. The son of a Boston saloonkeeper, Joe had cannily invested in everything from ship-building to movie production to buying the post-Prohibition rights to import British liquor. By 1929, he had established a $1 million trust fund for each of his eight children (His ninth and last child, Edward, was born 1932).

Later in life, he enthusiastically entered public service as the first head of the Securities and Exchange Commission and later as U.S. Ambassador to Great Britain. Joe, a notorious womanizer who once had an extra-marital affair with screen siren Gloria Swanson, among many others, encouraged a spirit of fierce competition among his brood. The Kennedy kids were forever vying for the best grades, fastest times in sailboat races, most touchdowns in touch football and driest quips at the dinner table.

JFK's devout mother Rose, daughter of boisterous Boston Mayor John F. (Honey Fitz) Fitzgerald, attended Roman Catholic Mass every day for 77 years. She instilled in her children a deep sense of Christian compassion and of duty to help the less fortunate.

With disturbing frequency, that faith was needed at home. JFK's eldest sister Rosemary, had been found to be mentally disabled. A botched lobotomy worsened her condition. She has spent most of her adult life in an institution, where she remains. For JFK's older brother, Joseph Jr., great things had been predicted. Upon his birth, grandpop Honey Fitz had summoned the

■ *In 1934, the Kennedys were a prolific clan of promise: (seated, from left) Patricia, Robert, mother Rose, Jack, baby Ted (on father Joe's lap); (standing, from left) Joe Jr., Kathleen, Rosemary, Jean and Eunice.*

Boston press to inform them that a future President of the United States was now in diapers. Joe did not survive World War II. Determined to prove his mettle after brother John's headline-making brush with the Japanese destroyer, Joe, a Navy flier, volunteered in 1944 to fly a plane stuffed with explosives and rigged to smash into its target like a winged bomb. Joe was supposed to bail out after aiming it at a German bunker inside France, but the plane exploded 20 minutes after takeoff. JFK's favorite sister Kathleen also died in a plane crash—in 1948, with her fiancé, a non-Catholic whom Joe Sr. and especially Rose disapproved of though he was a British Earl.

The three surviving Kennedy boys, Jack, Robert and Edward (Ted) pursued as their own their father's dream of a Democratic dynasty. They all attended Harvard before entering the sharp-elbowed world of Democratic politics.

∎BLACK JACK'S DARLING∎

Jacqueline Bouvier had emerged from a more sedate arena: Afternoon teas, riding to hounds and debutante balls. Her father, darkly handsome John (Black Jack) Bouvier III, whom Jackie and her sister, Lee, adored, was a hard-drinking flamboyant stockbroker, whose market plunges were as legendary as his sexual philandering. In summers the family sunned in stately homes and horse pastures in East Hampton, Long Island; come winter, they snuggled in their sprawling Park Avenue apartment. Jackie's mother, Janet, who prized her social standing, divorced Black Jack over his womanizing before Jackie was 12, and two years later married Hugh Auchincloss, a banker from a venerable, wealthy family.

Jackie was groomed to be a society wife. She attended Miss Porter's School in Farmington, Connecticut, a private finishing school, where young ladies, Jackie included, customarily kept their own horses in nearby stables. While Jackie sometimes seemed vague and at sea in new surroundings, she possessed a sharp wit and a first-rate mind. She made the dean's list at Vassar, before finishing her degree in French literature at George Washington University, in Washington, D.C.

∎COURTING, WITH SPARKS∎

JFK and Jackie met when he was a Congressman and she was working as an "inquiring photographer" for *The Washington Times-Herald*, the kind of job well-bred young women took in those days to meet men of influence. The two quickly became close. During their year-long engagement, Jackie endured weekends in Hyannis Port at the Kennedy compound (so called

"All my friends adored [my father]" Jackie once said of hard-drink-ing, philandering John "Black Jack" Bouvier III, with Jackie and her mother Janet at a Southampton, Long Island horse show in 1934.

because it comprises three houses spread over two-and-a-half acres). The family women, including matriarch Rose, found Jackie altogether too soft and vulnerable for the Kennedy brand of boisterous sibling rivalry.

For her part. Jackie found the Kennedys "terribly bourgeois," but gamely tried to fit in. She even braved the clan's all-out brand of touch football, until Teddy fell on her and broke her ankle during a scrimmage. She was, however, at complete ease with patriarch Joe. She spent hours talking with him, and often would nimbly argue with him. Joe was charmed. "She's the only one around here with any gumption," he said.

Nothing, however, better illustrates the differences between the Kennedys and the Bouvier-Auchinclosses than their disagreement over the 1953 wedding of Jack and Jackie. Janet Auchincloss wanted to restrict the guest list for her daughter's nuptials, to be held at the Auchincloss estate in Newport, Rhode Island, to an "intimate" 300 or so of the bluest bloods, press excluded. Joe Kennedy, already with an eye to his son's future run for the highest office, envisioned a grander affair marshalling a who's who of influential politicians and backers, with the press in full force. Joe won. Almost 1,000 attended the reception.

The newlyweds' relationship had jagged edges. As a congressman and senator, Jack was often away dealing with campaign and Kennedy family matters, leaving Jackie alone and lonely. Before Caroline was born, Jackie suffered a miscarriage and, within a year, a stillbirth.

Accustomed to the anything-goes hospitality his clan maintained at its summer duchy of Hyannis Port, Jack was liable to call Jackie at 11 a.m. and announce that he was bringing a couple dozen cronies home for lunch at their N Street home. She learned to keep the kitchen stocked.

Jackie had a harder time adjusting to one of JFK's other proclivities. According to most of his biographers, Kennedy filled his bachelor days with sexual conquests—coeds, secretaries, married women, even an occasional movie star, such as Gene Tierney. Marriage didn't slow him down. As President he dallied with Marilyn Monroe and with Judith Campbell, the girlfriend of a mafia don. Word of his betrayals filtered back to Jackie, producing tears and rows. Jackie once conceded, "I don't think there are any men who are faithful to their wives."

By the time they moved into the White House, the couple had found ways to accommodate each other. Youthful, telegenic JFK set about bringing his Boston "vigah" to Washington, to

"The handsome couple seemed the embodiment of youth," Arthur Schlesinger Jr. wrote of the Kennedys (at their wedding in 1953), "and rather daring in a nation ruled by old men."

develop what he called a "New Frontier" that ranged from a renewed concern for America's less fortunate to the creation of the Peace Corps, to an all-out push for landing a man on the moon. Jackie, who lent her intelligence and cosmopolitan style to the role of First Lady, had two priorities: Refurbish the fussy faded decor of the White House, and protect her children from a world that might otherwise turn them into spoiled brats.

■HELICOPTER HEAD■

From the moment he was able, as a toddler, to slip out of his crib himself and wobble past the stuffed-animal menagerie in his blue-and-white nursery, John Jr. displayed an innate sense of physical adventure. His Secret Service nickname was "Lark," for the way he could test agents' ability to keep up with him. The family called him "Helicopter Head," for his enchantment with his father's presidential chopper. Whenever it landed on the White House lawn, John would rush to meet his dad, sometimes spinning in imitation of the rotors, until he toppled giddily to the ground. One of his favorite toys was a model helicopter.

"I remember when he was about two years old," says Jackie's half-brother, Jamie Auchincloss, "not just going off the diving board and into the deep end of the swimming pool at Bailey's Beach in Newport, whether or not there was somebody right there to catch him. But actually asking for help to climb to the high diving board and just racing off the board to 10 feet of free fall. His father was often there to catch him."

One thing he was never called within the family was John-John. The nickname stuck with the American people, however, after a reporter overheard the President call twice quickly to his rambunctious son, "John, John!" In a 1996 interview on America Online, John said, "No one I know calls me John-John."

John loved exploring the First Family's 132-room residence. He spent hours marching like a soldier back and forth past the desk of his mother's secretary, Mary Barelli Gallagher. "Always," Gallagher wrote in her memoir *My Life with Jacqueline Kennedy*, "all the excitement within him would burst forward."

▪ LITTLE FEET IN THE OVAL OFFICE ▪

John and Caroline were the first children to bring the patter of little feet to the White House since 1893, when Grover Cleveland expanded his family in his second term. The Kennedy children were given free rein by their father, who had himself grown up in a large family in which children were underfoot at all times. Kennedy historian Arthur Schlesinger Jr. recalled to Jackie biographer Carl Sferrazza Anthony (*As We Remember Her*), "As [the President] sat down before his breakfast tray, surrounded by the morning papers and urgent cables and reports, Caroline and John would rush in, greet their father and turn on the television to watch animated cartoons."

JFK and Jackie had very different ideas about how the children should be raised. Jackie, who set up a nursery school in the third floor solarium of the White House, was determined that John and Caroline be allowed to grow up as unaffected as their unusual circumstances would allow. "Mrs. Kennedy was very strict about us staying away from [John Jr. and Caroline], letting them grow up normally," says retired Secret Service agent Robert W. Foster, who was one of the agents looking after the security of the Kennedy children. He often accompanied John on walks to Washington's Montrose Park for exercise and fresh air. Jackie, he said, "didn't want us hovering over them like a mother hen."

The President seemed refreshed by his children's exuberance. He often took John or Caroline with him on his way to work in the West Wing. And he would stop work when they came tearing into the Oval Office, and banter with them.

JFK was also a seasoned campaigner who understood that images of the vital young family could only help his Presidency. He once promised photographer Stanley Tretick (who died just three days after John Kennedy Jr.'s plane crashed) pictures of John playing in the Oval Office. The promise had to wait until Jackie—either on an official visit or vacationing—was out of the country. Tretick then snapped away at John crawling under his father's desk and cavorting in the head of state's chair. "President Kennedy wouldn't have done it if she had been there," Tretick once told a colleague. "I said to him, 'I bet you're the only President in history to bootleg his own kids.' And he just looked at me and smiled."

John's own memories of the White House were few. "We had a dog who was named Pushinka, who was given to my father by a Soviet official. And we trained that dog to slide down the slide we had in the back of the White House," he told CNN's Larry King in

1995. "Sliding the dog down that slide is probably my first memory."

He had a few precious recollections of his father. "I remember he used to call me Sam just to annoy me," Kennedy told Oprah Winfrey in a 1996 interview. "I remember getting kind of upset, you know. I'd say, 'My name is not Sam, it's John.' And he'd say, 'Oh, sorry, Sam.'"

As an adult, though, John was never sure about his life in the White House. "Sometimes I can't remember what really happened," he often told friends, "and what I saw in pictures." Former First Family photographer Jacques Lowe recalls that in 1995 Kennedy asked him to come to his office at *George*. "I hadn't seen him since he was a baby," says Lowe. "I expected that he wanted me to do some work for *George*. But I was showered with a barrage of questions about his father. He asked, 'How much time did I spend with him? What did he think of me? Did he ever bawl me out? What was his sense of humor like?' It was very emotional, but he wasn't crying or anything. He just wanted to know everything he could about JFK. Every little detail."

THE SADDEST SALUTE

Caroline and John were at home in the White House, about to take their nap, when the news reached their nanny Maud Shaw. Visiting Dallas on Nov. 22, 1963, JFK had been struck down by an assassin's bullet as he sat beside Jackie in an open limousine. Shaw told Caroline that their father was not coming home. John was told later.

Dressed in matching powder-blue coats and red shoes, John and Caroline attended their father's funeral three days later in St. Matthew's Cathedral in Washington, D.C. John, who turned three that day, got fidgety during the service. Jackie asked Secret Service man Foster to take the boy to a small room at the back of the cathedral. There, John was entertained by an Army colonel, who described to the curious boy what each of the medals on his uniform stood for. To thank the officer, John saluted him, something he had seen done countless times. But John used his left hand.

Recalls agent Foster: "The colonel said, 'Oh, no, John, that's not the way to salute. You salute with your right hand.' And he showed him how to salute properly. Then, when we went outside, I was standing right there, and Mrs. Kennedy said as the casket passed by, 'Say goodbye to your daddy, John,' and he whipped up that salute the right way, and I just about fell over. It wasn't coached or anything. He just did it."

In one heartbreaking moment seen around the world, John, who later said he had no memory of saluting, cemented his place in American lore. "That little boy saluting the casket," says Rev. Jesse Jackson, "touched something in our hearts."

THE BRAVEST BIRTHDAY PARTY

The Kennedys had a tradition of getting on with life in the face of any disaster. And so, after the official funeral reception at the

White House, Jackie and the children celebrated John's third birthday with a small party upstairs. Ted and Bobby Kennedy were there. Jackie lit the candles of the birthday cake. When it was time to sing "Happy Birthday," Bobby burst into tears and had to leave the room. Near the end of the party, he joined Teddy in singing a JFK favorite, "Heart Of My Heart."

Two weeks after the funeral, the family left the White House as Lyndon and Lady Bird Johnson moved in. John, however, was still not sure what had happened. Nanny Maud Shaw told him, "Your father has gone to heaven to look after Patrick," referring to the baby who had died four months earlier, after only two days of life, of the lung ailment that had bothered infant John. Thinking of Air Force One, which he loved, the boy asked her, "Did he take the big plane with him? I wonder when he's coming back?"

As preparations for moving were underway, agent Foster took John for one of their last walks outside. "I was getting him a drink out of the fountain," Foster recalls, "and a photographer came up and took some pictures. John looked him right in the eye and said, 'What are you taking my picture for? My daddy's dead.' The poor photographer started to cry. I cried too."

LIFE WITH JACKIE 3

Only one thing about the move from the White House visibly disturbed three-year-old John Kennedy. As he watched his toys being packed up, he became anxious that he would never see them again. So nanny Maud Shaw helped him set aside a selection of mechanical toys, guns and swords to carry with him. Wearing the beloved little Marine uniform he had been given, he waved a small American flag as the family bid their goodbyes.

Jackie kept up a brave front during the days following the assassination, but succumbed to bouts of depression at night. Just before Christmas of 1963 interior decorator Billy Baldwin visited the family to discuss the redecoration of their new home, a beige brick three story colonial town house in Georgetown, at 3017 N Street. Jackie's condition shocked him. Baldwin had done much of the White House restoration, as well as work on other Kennedy residences. She told the

> *"He was unspoiled and full of life and gaiety," says John H. Davis, author of* Jacqueline Bouvier: An Intimate Memoir, *who knew John (tanking up in 1963) later in New York City. "He liked to play hide and go seek."*

*"The world is pouring terrible adoration at the feet of my children,"
Jackie (rowing in Central Park with John and Caroline in 1964) told
her decorator Billy Baldwin. "How can I bring them up normally?"*

decorator that she felt "utterly alone. Can anyone possibly understand
how it is to have lived in the White House and then suddenly be living
alone as the President's widow? As First Lady, I made maybe two
friends."

In regard to her children, Jackie remained very clearheaded. Says
the former First Lady's social secretary, Letitia Baldrige, she "refused
to allow the children to be pampered." Recalls President Kennedy's
Press Secretary and family friend Pierre Salinger, "Only two days
after the assassination, Jackie came into my office to speak to me.
'Pierre,' she said, 'there is only one thing I can do now. I have to take
care of those kids day by day. I have to make sure they become intel-
ligent. I have to make sure they do good work in school. I have to
make sure when they get older that they have strong views on what
they should be doing. This is the only thing I can do any more.' "

■PIGGYBACK RIDES ON N STREET■

Many people visited the house to support her and her children.
Secret Service agent Robert Foster often showed up to play with
John. John sometimes called him "Daddy." According to biographer
Wendy Leigh, Jackie was disturbed about it and asked that the agent

be reassigned. Salinger, along with Secretary of Defense Robert McNamara and, of course, Bobby Kennedy, visited regularly to play with Caroline and John and take Jackie out to dinner.

Jackie became particularly close to Bobby, who would bring John to his office at the Justice Department. Jackie often travelled with the children to Hickory Hill—a Virginia estate that JFK had sold to Bobby and his wife, Ethel—where John and Caroline could play in the country with their cousins.

The President and Jackie had discussed what to do about the children if both parents should perish, and decided that John and Caroline should live with Bobby's family. After JFK's death, Jackie was adamant that her children spend more time at Hickory Hill, because she wanted them to have Bobby's "Kennedy" influence. She is quoted as saying by biographer Christopher Andersen in *Jackie After Jack*, "Jack made John the mischievous, independent boy he is. Bobby is keeping that alive."

Bobby and Ethel, as well as the rest of the clan, tried not to treat John and Caroline in a special way. "The Kennedys didn't put him on a pedestal or anything," says Barbara Gibson, who was Rose Kennedy's personal secretary.

Jackie didn't urge politics on the kids. "She didn't come from a political family...." John told *Today's* Katie Couric in May 1999. "She thought it was better to have a sense of who you are and your own place in life before you took [political life] on."

In the absence of a father, John became much more his mother's son. "He and his mother were very close," says Jamie Auchincloss, Jackie's half-brother. "They had a very strong mother-son bond." Jackie gently but firmly guided John's actions, and he responded by nearly always following her wishes. That didn't mean she was easy on him. Many years later John told a Florida waitress with whom he became friendly, "My mother was very strict with me. Caroline could do just about anything, but if I stepped out of line, I got a swat."

He also got certain indulgences. John had been smitten with airplanes since he learned to walk and talk. When he was five, Jackie, at great expense, presented him with him a beautifully reconditioned

World War II Piper Cub observation plane to clamber over.

While Jackie distanced herself from the Kennedy family influence, she never turned her back on their brand of athleticism. She seemed to look for situations in which John could prove himself. On an Hawaiian vacation in the '60s, the boy got caught in an undertow while swimming, and the Secret Service detail splashed in and pulled him ashore. Jackie thanked them, but according to Auchincloss, she told them, 'You're supposed to only protect him or Caroline against other people, and a mother has to remember what a mother has to do.' I think she was telling them not to worry in the future, that in case something happened and they couldn't get to him, she would be there for her son." She told the agents, "Drowning is my responsibility."

■ JACKIE'S KIND OF TOWN ■

There were, of course, many things she couldn't control. Jackie had hoped that, after leaving the White House, the family would lower its public profile. It was not to be. The N Street home became a regular stop on the Washington tourist route. Gawkers left lunch wrappers in the front yard, flashbulbs winked constantly and tour buses wheezed by. The Kennedys had to keep the shades drawn on the front of their house night and day.

The family escaped regularly for sojourns to the Kennedy enclaves in Hyannis Port and Palm Beach and winged to Aspen, Colorado to ski. But by 1964, the atmosphere in Washington was too oppressive. The Kennedy legacy seemed to loom everywhere, and politics was the only topic of conversation. With the help of her sister, Lee, Jackie left the capitol for the more cosmopolitan canyons of Manhattan, her childhood home. John, Caroline and Jackie were soon ensconced in an airy 15-room cooperative apartment at 1040 Fifth Avenue, between 85th and 86th Streets, where Jackie would live until her death in 1994. Lee and her husband, Stanislas Radziwill, lived just down the street at 969 Fifth Avenue. Also nearby were actor Peter

Jackie brought up John (skiing in Sun Valley in 1965) and Caroline so that, says Jackie biographer Nigel Hamilton, "They had their independent selves, their own personalities, and could stand aside from [the Kennedy influence]."

and wife Pat (Kennedy) Lawford and Steven and Jean Kennedy Smith, parents of John's favorite cousin, William.

The peripatetic John, sporting a Beatles-style mop (he did a wicked impression of the Fab Four), eagerly adapted. Jackie and a Secret Service agent walked John to St. David's School, a private Catholic institution for boys, for his first day of class in February 1965. He would spend happy years there, cementing a circle of friends including his cousin William Kennedy Smith. While they remained the most famous and recognizable children in America, John and Caroline began to enjoy more elbow room. John took tennis lessons in Central Park, across from the Kennedy apartment, and played soccer there with his classmates.

Caroline and John were ready to socialize more, but invitations to birthday parties and children's gatherings were few at first. Many parents dared not invite a Kennedy child to their homes, lest they be accused of social climbing or impertinence to a still-grieving family. When Jackie grasped the situation, she called the parents of classmates, assuring them that John and Caroline wanted to come to parties.

One of the few dark moments of his St. David's years occurred on the second anniversary of JFK's death. As John walked home from school with his mother, some boys began taunting, "Your father's dead! Your father's dead!" John quickly strode to his mother's side and firmly took her hand. It was as if, Jackie later said, "he were trying to assure me that things were all right. Sometimes it almost seems that he is trying to protect me instead of just the other way around."

The public's hunger for pictures and stories about the Kennedys never abated. Jackie waged her toughest New York battle against the increasingly bold tactics of the paparazzi. Photographer Ron Galella became the devil incarnate to Jackie. He once nearly knocked John off his bike when he jumped from behind a bush with his camera. During one holidays season, he hired someone to dress as Santa to hug Jackie, while he snapped away. Gallela eventually sued Jackie, claiming that Secret Service agents had broken his cameras. She counter-sued and won a restraining order against the photographer, requiring him to stay at least 25 feet away from Jackie and 30 feet away from her children.

▪LARK ON THE LOOSE▪

John rarely allowed these intrusions to cramp his emergence as a full-fledged, disco-age teenager. Sometimes he felt oppressed by his Secret Service shadows. Two agents accompanied him to school every day, and took turns napping while he attended classes. The coolest thing about them, John and his pals agreed, was that an agent was always willing to fetch pizzas during parties.

In 1968, the eight-year-old transferred to Manhattan's exclusive Collegiate School, a boy's institution. As he got older, he yearned to ditch his straitlaced minders, sneak off to Central Park to hang out or get into situations of which his mother would not approve. Joseph D'Angelo, who taught John at Collegiate, saw the bubbling exuberance. "Once when we were taking a trip to the Cloisters to look at medieval art," D'Angelo recalls, "we took the subway uptown. John had never been on a subway before and he was so excited. He had a million questions and was asking if he could open the window and hang his head outside. Afterwards, he was always on his mother's case to ride the subway alone with his friends."

Uncorraled, the young man did get himself into jams. On May 15, 1974, he eluded his security detail and pedaled his bike briskly into Central Park. An older teenager later identified as Robert Lopez, a heroin addict, leaped from behind a bush and yelled, "Get off that bike or I'll kill you!" John had taken boxing and karate lessons, but this was no time to practice. Lopez rode away on John's 10-speed. It is one of the ironies of John's legacy that Lopez, now an ex-con and an ex-junkie, later turned his life around with help from an organization funded in part by the Robin Hood Foundation, on which John served as a board member. Lopez turned 45 just days after John Kennedy's plane crashed.

Among his peers John tried to play down his celebrityhood, but there was no mistaking him for John Q. Public. Beck Lee, a New York public relations executive who was a close friend of Victoria Lawford, Peter and Pat Kennedy Lawford's daughter, often saw John at parties. "He wasn't at all really an awkward teenager," says Lee. "He had a commanding presence. He'd come in to a party with his own group of five or six girls and boys. He used words like 'cool' and was casually dressed. He would be in the center of his own party. But he was never too talkative. He had a sort of rock star quietness about him that I later thought may have come from the layers of protection that surrounded him."

Rock star ego trips cut no ice with school-minded Jackie. Collegiate's D'Angelo once got a call from Jackie over a ship-to-shore telephone. She and the children were cruising in the Mediterranean, but the mail had caught up with them. "I had written John a note saying he had not done his homework," explains D'Angelo, "and she said I could be certain he would have his homework in and that, if not, not to speak to anybody else but her. That was absolutely typical of everything she did."

"If you bungle raising your children," Jackie once said, "I don't think whatever else you do matters very much." According to John, she never faltered. "She took a lot of pride in being a good mother," he told *Today's* Katie Couric in May 1999. "And I'm glad people think it worked."

IDYLL IN GREECE

The year 1968 provided wrenching twists in the unending saga of the Kennedys, and neither they nor the country were ever the same. The Democratic convention in Chicago that summer was an unseemly affair at which riot-helmeted police cracked the scruffy heads of young protesters burning draft cards, American flags, or just bridges across the generation gap. Kennedy family friend Frank Mankiewicz, who was Robert Kennedy's press secretary, observes that JFK's assassination "changed us. We became angrier, abrasive, furious and quick to violence."

Encouraged by his family, and invigorated by his stint as Attorney General in his brother's administration, Robert Kennedy was running for President. Jackie made campaign appearances for him, and her children were excited about their uncle's new status. But following a speech on June 5 in Los Angeles celebrating his victory in the

"He was rough and simple but magnetic," a friend recalled of Aristotle Onassis (with John and Jackie in New York City in 1969). He also proved to be an effective stepfather to Jackie's children almost until his death in 1975.

37

California Democratic primary, he was fatally shot by a Jordanian immigrant, Sirhan Sirhan.

For Jackie, seeing Bobby laid to rest beside JFK in Arlington was the last straw. "If they're killing Kennedys," she said, "then my children are targets."

"Jacqueline was utterly devastated by it," says Jackie's cousin, John H. Davis, author of *Jacqueline Bouvier: An Intimate Memoir.* "She wanted to get out of this country at all costs. She almost gave up on America all together."

▪A SUITABLY POWERFUL SUITOR▪

Cruel and cutting, the joke flourished around water coolers and at cocktail parties in the summer of 1968.

John Kennedy: My mother calls you the Frog.
Aristotle Onassis: Why is that?
John Kennedy: Because she says when you croak, we'll be rich!

Four months after Bobby's murder, Jackie married the world's richest man, shipping magnate Aristotle Onassis, on his private Greek island, Skorpios. Jackie had been acquainted with Ari, as he was called, since 1957. After Jackie's infant son Patrick died in 1963, her sister Lee, who also knew Onassis, convinced Jackie, who was still First Lady, to cruise the Mediterranean with her on his yacht, *Christina.* Jackie joined sis, Lee, and Lee's husband Prince Stanislas Radziwill for the two-week excursion.

Ari, the son of a Turkish tobacco merchant, amassed a fortune of $500 million through canny deals and sometimes sheer muscle. By 29, he was a millionaire from marketing his own brand of cigarettes. With that money, he bought oil tankers during the depression, and later diversified his investments. In the mid-'60s, Ari began a sophisticated, diamond-sprinkled courtship of the former First Lady. He was attentive and kind to Jackie, and moved in a glittering circle of friends. By 1968, she was ready to marry him. The Kennedy clan

Jackie (leaving Central Park with her son in 1969) instilled in John, "just sort of living your life and doing what you feel, and where your interests take you," he told Larry King in 1995.

objected. It might derail Bobby's presidential chances. So Jackie agreed to wait until after the November election.

Speculation surrounded the relationship. Was Jackie marrying for money? Money, it was true, would no longer be a concern for her: After intense prenuptial conferences directed by Ted Kennedy, Onassis agreed to pay Jackie $3 million before the wedding, and established a million-dollar trust fund for her children. Was Jackie in love? "My sister needs a man like Onassis," said Lee, "who can protect her from the curiosity of the world."

Despite her yearning for privacy Jackie informed Onassis that for nine months of the year she would reside in New York City. That was where her children attended school.

While Onassis appreciated Jackie's elegance and wit, he may have seen her as another of his many prize acquisitions. He had been an international playboy and numbered among his pals Eva Péron, Greta Garbo, and Richard Burton and Elizabeth Taylor. The great

love of the widower's life, aside from his teenage children, Christina and Alexander, was the famously tempestuous opera diva Maria Callas. Their involvement continued hot and cold throughout his marriage to Jackie.

■THE PRINCE'S NEW PLAYGROUND■

For John Kennedy Jr., his mother's remarriage delivered fairly conflict-free rewards. A vast floating playground, Onassis's 322-foot ocean-going yacht, *Christina*, was as grand as the White House. The ship boasted nine luxury suites, gold bathroom fixtures and a dance floor that drew back to reveal a swimming pool. It boarded a crew of 60, including hairdressers, chefs and even a masseuse.

More importantly, Onassis treated John and Caroline like his own children. An inveterate walker in any port-of-call, Ari would often take John along on his strolls and talk to him over dinner in local bistros.

John found the rugged, sun-baked island of Skorpios charming. Onassis gave the boy—seven years old at the time of the wedding—his own battery-powered Jeep and a sleek red speedboat with his name in script on the front. John got on well with Alexander Onassis, who was some 10 years older (Alexander was killed in a plane crash in 1973; Christina died of heart failure in 1988). Alexander, who, like his sister, never approved of their father's marriage, nonetheless enjoyed ocassionally playing with John and Caroline.

▪LEARNING ABOUT DADDY▪

Though Jackie had her misgivings about the Kennedys, she did not want her children to lose touch with their family heritage. In the summer of 1972, she persuaded Pierre Salinger, Kennedy's former press secretary, to sail on *Christina*. "I want you to spend an hour or an hour and a half a day with John Jr. and Caroline and explain everything about what their father did," she told him.

Salinger responded passionately, relating vivid narratives of JFK in World War II, Congress, the Senate and the White House. "The kids were very excited about all the things I told them," he says, "because they had not had that kind of information about their father. I think it got something important in their brains about their future."

The Greek idyll ended badly, however. Jackie, increasingly upset about her husband's flamboyant lifestyle and his criticism of her spending, would not let Ari stay with her when he came to New York City. As the situation escalated, they took pains to avoid even being in the same city at the same time. Onassis was reluctantly contemplating divorce when he died of myasthenia gravis in 1975. Jackie eventually received some $26 million from his estate, ensuring her and her children's financial future.

The day before Onassis's funeral, Jackie flew to Skorpios. Her mother, Janet Auchincloss, Caroline and John met her at the airport. Paparazzi popped up everywhere, and the family, once again left without a husband and father, was besieged by reporters. John, then 15, clutching a rolled-up comic book, stuck out his tongue at a photographer—a gesture that would, achingly, be echoed 22 years later by his 11-year-old niece, Rose, leaving the scene of his own memorial service in New York City.

GROWING UP

Finally! He was out of the house, away from the prying press, searching for his own place in the world. John was on his way to prep school, with Caroline already at Harvard. Jackie was relaxing somewhat her single-minded vigilance. In 1975, she became a part-time book editor at Viking Press, later moving to Doubleday to become a full-time editor.

John could relax a bit, too. He was hardly the first celebrity to attend Phillips Academy in Andover, Massachusetts. The ivy-covered walls of one of the oldest private preparatory schools in the U.S. had housed George Washington's nephews. Oliver Wendell Holmes, George Bush and Jack Lemmon, among other notables, had passed beneath its soaring white spires. One of John's classmates was actor-to-be James Spader, who became a pal.

Of course, none of those well-bred boys had come to Andover drag-

▩ *"He was Young America," says Jackie's designer Oleg Cassini of John (in Boston in 1979). "He had gotten rid of all the pomposity and all the ceremony and he was trying to live an American life... and he succeeded."*

43

■ *"He drove his own car and flew his own plane," Ted Kennedy said in his eulogy of John (revving up at his mother's New Jersey estate in 1975), "which is how he wanted it. He was king of his domain."*

ging the baggage of being America's most famous teen, complete with bodyguards in sunglasses. At first, other students shied from the wattage. But the young Kennedy, who was to spend 11th and 12th grade at Andover, as Phillips is commonly called, easily melded with his 1,200 fellow students. "It felt more like he didn't have to try to blend in," says Meredith Price, who was a house master of Stearns West Hall during John's tenure. "He just did blend in because of his nature."

John, whose predilections were more preppy than posh, grew the full sideburns fashionable at the time, sprouted a sensuous uncombed mop, and fell happily into sync with the school's no-code dress code. He'd show up to play hard-contact Ultimate Frisbee in an unironed Brooks Brothers button-down, drooping khaki shorts and deck shoes, no socks. He sported his own set of wheels—an ever-present skateboard.

Rooming in Stearns West with 21 other boys, John was situated on the shores of Rabbit Pond, an infamous body of water into which, legend has it, a young Humphrey Bogart tossed a teacher during his brief career as an Andover student. John's room was just like everyone else's—messy—except for one detail. "It was a very humbling experience for me to walk in the room," Price says, "and there was a wonderful picture of John and his father together."

■SOMETHING NEW: THE BUS■

JFK Jr. had never lived without the Secret Service on the periphery. But when he was 16 that protection—the pampering assistance, Jackie notwithstanding, as well as the bothersome hovering—was, by a House resolution, lifted. No more free rides in the imposing limos with tinted windows. Suddenly, to travel to the family compound in Hyannis Port, John had to ride the bus from Andover to Boston's South Station, where he was met by a family driver.

John found normalcy novel. Kennedys traditionally don't deal with money as most folks do. They rarely carry cash. John asked house master Price for a loan. Price's father-in-law, a staunch Republican, was visiting. Kennedy had never met the man, but confessed he was out of money and wondered if he could borrow five dollars. "So my father-in-law let him borrow the money," Price says. "He died a few years later, and he was probably smiling about the fact that John Kennedy never paid him back."

Academically, John Jr. proved very much his father's son. At preppy Choate, Jack had failed French and Latin, before his father and his teachers cracked the whip. Jackie, says family friend, author Edward Klein, "was concerned that John wasn't living up to his potential." Although Jackie often encouraged her son by phone and

Kennedy caught a wave in Jamaica at 16, in 1977. He never met an individual sport he didn't like. Okay, maybe shuffleboard.

mail and sent him care-packages of cookies, he missed classes and at one point fell so far behind that he was unable to pass one of Andover's rigorous final exams. According to biographer Wendy Leigh, when asked by the press if he considered himself a good student, John replied, "Well, I don't know. It depends on what you call a poor student."

Failing a final at Andover always means "remedial action." In John's case, he was allowed to stay for another year of smoke and sweat.

Book learning took a back seat to other interests as well. In the mellow '70s, the aroma of marijuana smoke wafted through campuses across the nation, and Andover was no exception. John had smoked pot at Collegiate, according to a classmate, and even in the family apartment. Later at Andover, John was caught by campus security guards sharing a joint with fellow students. John didn't deny it, or try to explain it away. Despite the "reckless seam that ran deep through the Kennedy nature," said biographer Leigh, "he had a powerful inner compass that ultimately steered him away from excess."

Taking a page from the Kennedy philosophy, Jackie decided that physical challenge would get her son back on track. So during summers of his Andover years he embarked, at her instigation, on rugged adventures. In the summer of '76, John and cousin Timothy Shriver dug trenches and built outhouses in a Guatemalan village that had been leveled by an earthquake. July '77 found him on an Outward Bound wilderness survival course on a bleak island off the Maine coast.

The next summer John irrigated pastures, herded cows and strung barbed wire on the Wyoming cattle ranch of John Perry Barlow, once a lyricist for the Grateful Dead, and now a busy activist for Internet freedom of speech. Barlow's ranch had been recommended to Jackie by a Wyoming congressman, and according to Barlow, Jackie "wanted him to get out and around, get in closer contact with the salt of the earth and get his hands on something real." Volunteering in Andover's community service program, John also taught English to immigrant children of middle-school age in the economically depressed city of Lawrence, Mass.

▪FLOURISHING AT BROWN▪

Brown University was a surprising choice for John. His father, his uncles and his sister had all gone to Harvard. But John, Jackie agreed, had enough on his plate without having to compete with ghosts and a crackerjack sibling. And indeed John found his academic footing at Brown perhaps more easily than he would have at Harvard. He took a seminar on the Vietnam War, during which he asked Jackie and the Kennedys for resource material, and arranged for Jackie's friend, documentary filmmaker Peter Davis, to screen his Vietnam opus *Hearts and Minds* in class.

John and his friend Charlie King, now a New York City attorney, formed a discussion group with a few fellow Brown students in a side room in the dining hall. They would argue the issues of the day: evolution vs. creationism, affirmative action, arms control, civil rights. Says King: "John had definite opinions on things, but he also argued on both sides of the issue. He was definitely passionate about civil rights. John was very adamant about the fact that we had to have equal rights for everybody in our society."

Novelist Rick Moody *(The Ice Storm)* registered as a freshman at Brown University in the fall of 1979 and heard the buzz during orientation—John Kennedy was on campus. After John's death, Moody recalled his first Kennedy sighting in *The New Yorker*: "A tall, perfectly handsome guy in jeans and a Hawaiian shirt; a smile like a million bucks ... I saw the most famous teenager on earth get seconds of pizza."

Even though, as at Andover, other famous offspring were enrolled—among the undergraduates on the Providence, Rhode Island, campus were Walter Mondale's son, William, and John's own cousin Kerry Kennedy—none had the magnetism of JFK Jr. Brown's spacious, open-access commons and metropolitan environs spelled opportunity for the paparrazi, who had been held at bay outside the more bucolic campus at Andover. Motor-drives whirred as the fledgling American History major stood in line to register for his first courses. John found the swarm irritating, he would confide to friends, but he never lost his cool.

Making friends quickly, John entered easily into the life of the school. He good-naturedly weathered the sophomoric ritual of fraternity hazing, emerging as a full-fledged Phi Kappa Psi. "He was a pretty upbeat guy," says his fraternity brother Richard Wiese, a New York City freelance newscaster. "People gravitated towards him."

Girls couldn't get enough, and John's telephone number was not listed in the campus directory. "He was used to a lot of women who would melt in front of him," says Wiese, noting that John was turned off by anyone who put on social airs. The fraternity did capitalize on his babe-attracting power, though. Women would come from other schools for a weekend of Brown parties; Phi Psi once hung up a sign announcing that JFK Jr., was on hand. Lines to get in snaked down the block.

Jackie visited her son occasionally. And took John's friend Wiese by surprise. "John and I were sitting on the wall of the fraternity," recalls Wiese, "and he said 'I forgot I have to hand in my paper. Can you wait here for my Mom? You know what she looks like—dark hair, dark glasses.'

"I introduced myself to her, and she asked to see his room. He and his roommate had the sloppiest room in the frat and she needed to use the phone and she couldn't see the phone. She was down on her hands and knees on the floor, following the wire through the clothes—and it turned out to be a stereo wire. She ended up visiting my room to use the phone, and she told him that my room was neater."

Another time, Wiese reluctantly let the free-and-easy Kennedy wear his blazer to a dinner—they were the same size. A food fight erupted, and Wiese's jacket was stained. John assured him he'd have the coat cleaned. "Three weeks later," says Wiese with a smile, "I saw it behind the couch, all rolled up in a ball, and he still hadn't taken it to the laundry. But you couldn't get mad at him. Sure, you cut him more slack than most people, but he grew up with a lot more people yessing him."

At times John seemed to enjoy being the butt of practical jokes. One night, as he was leaving the Phi Psi house made up for a play he was appearing in, some pals waiting for him let fly water balloons, splashing his theatrical costume. "He took it all in real good stride," says Rick Guy, now corporation counsel for the City of Syracuse. "He just ran back upstairs and cleaned himself up. It's not as if he started yelling or swearing at anyone. He was obviously perturbed but he didn't verbalize it. He was a classy guy."

■THE ACTOR IN HIM■

In a sense, John Kennedy Jr. had been on stage since he was born. He became adept early at presenting himself appealingly to the ever-present cameras. At Andover, John acted in three plays, but his romance with the grease paint blossomed at Brown. During his undergraduate years, he appeared in *The Tempest, The Playboy of The Western World*, Ben Jonson's *Volpone*, and Miguel Pinero's *Short Eyes*. He hacked his hair to a brutal buzz to play a dangerous street hood in David Rabe's *In The Boom Boom Room*, and was gratified that strangers in Providence failed to recognize him in his new 'do.

Could he be a contenda? Luckily he was saddled with neither the Boston-Irish drawl of the Kennedys nor the thoroughbred tones of his mother's New York and Connecticut set. Novelist Moody, who also had a role in *In The Boom Boom Room*, wrote that John "imbibed the Method without ever having set foot in the Actor's Studio," echoing the approach of Brando and Nicholson among others.

John was seriously thinking about becoming an actor. He had a star's charisma, no doubt. Although Jackie had attended many of John's performances, she was dead-set against his making a career of it. She told him once, "You can act, or you can be."

"Jackie made it clear that John was the standard bearer of Camelot. She didn't want him to act," says Kennedy biographer Christopher Andersen.

Jackie was a persuasive person. "When you got anywhere near Jackie," says her half-brother Jamie Auchincloss, "you didn't think about anything but Jackie. She sucked all of the oxygen out of the air for 100 miles around. Her strength was, you didn't get into any arguments with her and you never said no. Nobody did."

■ *John, courtside in 1977 with one of his summer squeezes, Meg Azzoni, attracted girls because of "his humor and easy-going manner," says author Carl Sferrazza Anthony.*

And so, on June 6, 1983, as John took his place with his graduating class of 1,400, wearing white chinos and cowboy boots under his gown, he smiled and waved to his mother sitting among other proud parents. His acting days were virtually over.

A MAN OF HIS CLAN

E.B. White, that cogent codger, author of *Char-lotte's Web* and a seacoast loving New Englander himself, once wrote these lines about John F. Kennedy Sr., but he could have been speaking of the president's son: "He never feared the weather ... instead he challenged the wind, to change its direction and to cause it to blow more kindly and more softly over the world and its people."

John Jr. was ever a Kennedy, whether he was playing football or working unseen to help the indigent. While some friends believe John would have taken the leap at some point, he was ever ambivalent about the political arena. "If your father was a doctor and your uncles are doctors and all your cousins are doctors and all the family ever talks about is medicine, there's a good chance maybe you're going to be a doctor too," he said in 1993.

■ *Of life with his father, John would tell friends, "Sometimes I can't remember what really happened and what I saw in pictures." In 1977, he broke ground for the JFK Memorial Library with Rose Kennedy (in hat), Teddy and Jackie.*

"But maybe you want to be a baker." In 1994 he explained, "Once you run for office, you're in it. Sort of like going into the military. You'd better be damned sure it is what you want to do and that the rest of your life is set up to accommodate that. It takes a certain toll on your personality and on your family life. I've seen it personally. So if I were to do it, I would make sure that was what I wanted to do and that I didn't do it because people thought I should."

His uncle, Senator Ted Kennedy, was one of the people who thought he should, and enlisted John's help in several political campaigns. In the summer of 1981, when John worked at a Washington think tank called the Center for Democratic Policy, Uncle Ted encouraged John to hold a press conference as a way of showcasing his positions. Instead, John showcased his charm: With a nod to his ink-stained white shirt, he quipped, "I would wear one of those plastic pocket protectors, but they make you look like a Republican."

New York lawyer Charlie King, a fellow Brown University student who was working on Ted Kennedy's presidential campaign in 1980, asked John to speak at a campaign event to be held at nearby Providence College. "I thought it was going to be a small gathering of folks in Rhode Island," recalls King. "It would be a few volunteers getting together, so he said he'd do it. When we got over there, the parking lot we were told to go to was filled with cars and I was going, 'This is really odd.' All the state's political heavyweights were wedged in among 800 people in the auditorium. And then they announced, 'And now we're going to hear from John Kennedy!' John had nothing prepared. John didn't say anything about this until years later [in the '90s], and he said, 'The most embarrassing experience I ever had publicly was that. All I could think about is, Charlie King, you're dead.' It was his first real public speech and he wasn't even prepared for it."

John felt similarly overwhelmed at a 1988 appearance at Bloomingdale's in Manhattan, where he was to promote a line of Christmas tree ornaments designed by handicapped people to benefit

■ *John (flanked by RFK sons RFK Jr., left, and Christopher Kennedy at the 1990 wedding of their sister, Kerry, to Andrew Cuomo) "was more of a steady type" than a "rowdy" like Bobby's kids, says Bob Mann, a former aide to Ted.*

the Very Special Arts charity started by his aunt Jean Kennedy Smith in 1974. The ensuing crush was so bad that an electrician had to shut down an escalator to slow the throngs. "We didn't want it to turn out the way it did," admitted a staffer for Very Special Arts. "It was very obnoxious from the second he walked in. John hoped it would be more substantive."

He tried to harness that star power on behalf of his Uncle Ted's political campaigns, but simultaneously tried not to outshine Senator Kennedy. Campaigning in East Boston in 1994, for instance, John found himself fielding questions about whether he himself should run. "Not this time around," he told the voters. "Vote for

■ *John (in a family scrimmage in Hyannis Port in 1997) played touch football in New York City's Central Park for 15 years, says his former Brown University fraternity brother Richard Wiese.*

Teddy." Commenting on the hubbub, he sighed, "I think they're at the wrong rally." As his friend Charlie King points out, "The allure of being a senator wasn't one that drove him. What motivated him was making a difference."

Perhaps the most resonant moment for John since his heartbreaking salute at his father's funeral was when he introduced Uncle Ted in a brief 1988 speech at the Democratic National Convention in Atlanta. "Over a quarter century ago," Kennedy said then, "my father stood before you to accept the nomination for the Presidency of the United States. So many of you came into public service because of him. In a very real sense, because of you, he is with us still. And for that, I'm grateful to all of you."

John was welcomed with a two-minute standing ovation, and another followed when he was finished. "It was fantastic," says Pierre Salinger. "I was telling him that this speech showed

strongly that John Jr. should start thinking about going into politics. He said he was interested but he was still too young. He told
me that he had an idea that he should go into politics in the next
century."

▪WHAT HE COULD DO FOR HIS COUNTRY▪

John always kept in mind a favorite passage from Luke 12:48
often quoted by his grandmother Rose: "Of everyone to whom
much has been given, much will be required." He was still a
teenager when he realized he could give back quietly by pursuing
another Kennedy tradition: charity. In the summer of 1976, when
he was only 15, he went to Guatemala to aid earthquake victims;
in 1979, he attended National Outdoor Leadership School to
study environmental issues on Mount Kenya; in the summer of
1980, he met with student and government leaders in Zimbabwe
and after traveling to apartheid-torn South Africa to work for a
mining company, he formed the South African Group for Education, a campus lecture series designed to draw attention to the
country's injustices. In 1982, during the summer after his junior
year at Brown, he spent six weeks teaching English to low-income
teens in a University of Connecticut program, and after graduating
from Brown in 1983 he went to India to study public health and
food production, and to tutor children in the slums of Delhi. He
continued the Kennedy legacy of civil rights work by researching
the issue as a law clerk with the Justice Department in 1987, and
from 1988 to 1990 he helped develop the Mental Retardation and
Developmental Disabilities Studies Program, which awarded fel-
lowships funded by the Joseph P. Kennedy Jr. foundation.

Perhaps his signature charity was Reaching Up, a nonprofit
organization he founded in 1989 to benefit workers who cared for
the mentally disabled. "Now it has about 1000 people who take
classes and over 400 Kennedy fellows who get extra scholarship
money and career mentoring, and each one of them has met

■ *John, playing papoose with Uncle Teddy on the slopes of Stowe, Vermont in 1964 at age 3, would later supplement Ted as a kind of "assistant uncle" to John's younger cousins, recalls Bob Mann.*

John," the group's executive director Bill Ebenstein said after Kennedy's death. But Kennedy often insisted that Reaching Up leave his name out of its press releases, fearing he would distract from its mission. In 1991, Kennedy joined the board of the Robin Hood Foundation, a New York City group that fights poverty with after-school and food programs and job training. He was a member of President Clinton's Committee on Mental Retardation and was helping to organize a presidential conference on the relationship between poverty and disability.

In keeping with his sense of family continuity, John accepted invitiations to sit on the boards of the JFK Library Foundation and the Institute of Politics at the JFK School of Government at Harvard (when Teddy suggested to John that he should head the Institute, the younger man said he hoped to broaden its purpose beyond campaign and legislation issues). Together with his sister Caroline, John organized the Profile in Courage Award given out annually since 1989 at his father's presidential library in Boston. In fact, the Monday after his fateful flight to Martha's Vineyard, he had an appointment with Paul Newman and author A. E. Hotchner to plan an awards ceremony to honor philanthropic-minded companies. "He's very intent on doing only things he's qualified to do," a colleague at the Institute of Politics said in 1995. "He really wants to be involved."

▪ BLOOD TIES ▪

Like most of his family members, John believed in doing his best to keep the Kennedy flag flying, even under the barrage of ugly publicity that followed when his cousin William Kennedy Smith, a close friend since childhood, was accused of rape in Palm Beach, Fla., in 1991. Kennedy attended jury selection for Smith's trial "to show support" for Smith and discuss strategy, recalls Smith's lawyer, Roy Black. (Smith was acquitted.) "He said he was absolutely convinced that Will was innocent of what he was charged with, that it was totally out of character, and that he didn't believe it for a minute," Black recalls.

"We grew up together," Kennedy told reporters at the time. "I thought I could at least come down and be with him during some difficult times." That showed courage, says Black: "I think it was an extraordinary act on John's behalf because he had to know how much attention and publicity that would draw to him." John even scolded reporters, "I don't think any of you have been fair to my cousin." Despite the acquittal, the case rubbed more gloss off the family crest. "It's too much to ask anyone, even John, to live up to the Kennedy legacy," his friend Mary Anne Grafton-Rodgers, a Democratic activist, told PEOPLE in 1995, "because it's 90 percent myth."

But if Kennedy was loyal to Smith and devoted to his family, when he became a journalist at the helm of *George* he had no problem putting objectivity ahead of family ties. Famously, he once used its pages to chide his cousins Joseph P. Kennedy and Michael Kennedy, and as editor, he sat down for an interview with his father's archenemy Fidel Castro for an article that never ran and invited *Hustler* publisher Larry Flynt to a White House Correspondent's dinner. Flynt told *New York*, "There was a person, once, who attempted to sabotage our friendship, asking him how he could be friends with the man who published nude photographs of his mother in *Hustler* in 1975. His response was, 'I'm a Kennedy. I'm thick-skinned.'"

"MANAGEABLE DANGER"

A big part of being a Kennedy involved demonstrating what his father had so appealingly called "vigah." By age 2½ John was horseback riding with instructor Herb Spector, who says, "considering his age, he was very much at ease around animals. He didn't show any fear at all."

Kennedy grew up to be a one-man workout highlight reel, often chasing down Frisbees or footballs in Central Park, biking or in-line skating to work. His Uncle Bobby had taught him to ski, and John kept racking up new activities—snowboarding, ice-climbing, rock-climbing, helicopter skiing, sea-kayaking, paragliding, scubadiving and, of course, flying. In 1999, he even asked National Park officials for permission to rappel down Mount Rushmore. (They politely declined.) Eric Stiller, who gave Kennedy kayaking lessons at Pier 63 in Manhattan, says that the former president's son had "a soft type of hubris, an innate feeling that assumes you can do any physical task. And if you have a problem, you'll figure it out once you get into it. When my dad and I showed John how to put [a folding sea kayak] together and take it apart, I got the feeling that this was not a guy who takes a lot of time to be pre-

▪ *After John's rousing introduction of candidate Ted at the 1988 Democratic National Convention in Atlanta, former JFK Sr. aide Pierre Salinger told him, "I'm excited about your speech, and I want you to be President."*

pared. He wanted to take personal control of the situation right away."

Kennedy approached risking his neck in the spirit of his old Secret Service nickname: Lark. Ralph Diaz, editor of *The Folding Kayak* newsletter and an acquaintance of Kennedy's, says, "He showed what I consider an overly casual approach to kayaking on the water." Diaz once saw Kennedy go out on the Hudson River without such safety equipment as a life jacket or a bilge pump, and says Kennedy seemed oblivious to the potentially dangerous summer weekend boating traffic. "As I watched him paddling the day we had the talk on folding kayaks, I said to myself that this guy is going to get himself hurt one day, paddling the way he did [without taking precautions]."

Kennedy himself described in an article he wrote in *The New York Times* how he went with three pals in search of "manageable danger" on a 1991 kayaking trip to the Aland archipelago between Sweden and Finland. And danger he found: the Baltic Sea, he noted, "can quickly turn mean," and as waves slammed the kayakers' chests, a friend capsized into the 50-degree water and was forced to cling to the back of Kennedy's kayak while John struggled to keep his balance and drift ashore.

Later in the trip, as Kennedy left the shelter of an island, he recalled, "the wind lifted my paddle and threw it over my head, nearly capsizing me." Two of his friends did indeed capsize, and swam to shore. "They ran into a typical novice accident," says Diaz.

Kennedy had aided a friend in need on an earlier trip as well. Barry Clifford, a pal and diving companion, told *New York* that Kennedy had calmly rescued a third man, John Beyer, when the three were scuba-diving into the hulk of a sunken World War I freighter off Martha's Vineyard in the early '80s. Beyer's regulator broke, denying him oxygen, so "Kennedy immediately gave Beyer his regulator and they buddy-breathed," Clifford said. "But it wasn't just a simple buddy-breathing where you had to get to the surface. We had to go through these passageways that were falling down—like going through a maze—to get out of the ship. But John didn't even blink. There was no panic. It was just cool, calm, collected, business as usual."

Kennedy seemed to take such feats in stride. "He had an incredible physical prowess and amazing stamina," says Hilary Shepard-Turner, a close friend of Kennedy's girlfriend of five years, Daryl Hannah. "We would go skiing all day in Telluride [Colorado], and everyone else would collapse. Then he would go on a two-hour bike ride through the mountains. Seriously."

FOOTBALL, KENNEDY STYLE

If there is an official sport of the Kennedy family, it is touch football, and John, who even found time for a quick game on his wedding day, always played to win. Fraternity brother Richard Wiese makes John sound like the Ernie Banks of touch football: "We used to play Saturday mornings in Central Park. We did it for 15 years. He'd call up at eight or nine in the morning and say, 'It's a great day' and 'There's a blue sky' and we'd say, 'John, it's 20 degrees out.' He also had his own set of Kennedy rules. The first time I played at the compound, they played a game called 'Razzle Dazzle,' in which, for example, on a kickoff you could throw a forward pass."

Adds another pal, Charlie King, "He had a competitive streak in him when he was playing sports. There was one time [on the football field] when he knocked me almost unconscious. It was a basic random pick-up game, but I got the message. It was a jarring hit. I felt like all the bones in my body had been shattered. The play before it, I had broken up a pass that was going to John. Then when we got the ball on the next play, when I was trying to catch the pass, he didn't really try to block the pass, he just knocked the s--- out of me." As another old friend, Frank Mankiewicz, puts it, "He grew up with the notion that life has to be lived to the fullest. He didn't shrink or hang back from experience."

7

CAROLINE

"*My family photo* album," John Kennedy Jr. once mused, "is shared by a lot of people." For John, that album begins endearingly, with his big sister leaning over his crib to kiss him at the behest of a photographer when he was weeks old. "I just know he's going to be my birthday present," Caroline said, and her brother arrived on Thanksgiving, November 25, 1960, two days before her own third birthday. Sadly, both children's birthdays fell within days of their father's assassination.

Growing up in the White House, where Caroline rode her pony Macaroni on the lawn, big sister let little brother know who knew best. Recalls Barbara Gibson, Rose Kennedy's personal secretary from 1968 to 1977, "Caroline was always after him. 'John, do this.' And, 'You're not supposed to do that, John.'" Boss Caroline was also the first of the Kennedy kids to march into a press conference, announcing solemnly to one gathering of reporters that her

Caroline (dancing with her brother at cousin Michael's 1981 wedding) "is private in a healthy way," says Kennedy biographer Laurence Leamer. "There's a very self-protective way about her."

daddy was "upstairs with his shoes and socks off, doing nothing."

Unlike her brother, who was mercifully too little to absorb the horror of his father's murder, Caroline harbored detailed and painful memories. "She comprehended the assassination fully, absolutely," said her childhood French teacher, Jacqueline Hirsh, in an oral history. "She just looked ghastly."

"Caroline withdrew into herself. Maybe she was more sensitive," said Jackie's cousin John H. Davis, author of *Jacqueline Bouvier: An Intimate Memoir*. "JFK Jr. didn't even know his father. He has no recollection of him. She's probably devastated [even] today." Their mother took both children to their father's grave in Arlington National Cemetery on May 29, 1964, on what would have been the president's 47th birthday. The children knelt quietly together—in the same spot where they would bend down to kiss their mother's coffin in 1994.

▪ THICKER THAN WATER ▪

After their father's death, John became increasingly more adventurous than his sister. On a 1965 trip to London, John climbed on the cannons at the Tower of London and yelled out to his sister, "Come on, Caroline. Let's crawl through here," but his sister held back. "It's a bit dirty," she replied.

Despite their divergent temperaments, the two always stayed close. "You never had to urge him to be kind to his sister," said their nanny Maud Shaw, "since he shared things with her and remembered her when he was given anything." Caroline captured John's mischevious sense of fun, as well as her own devotion to him, in a poem she penned as a Christmas present for their grandmother Rose Kennedy in 1971. It read in part:

He comes spitting in my room jabbing left and right
Shouting, OK, Caroline ready for a fight.
He is trying to blow us up with his chemistry set,
He has killed all the plants but we've escaped as yet.
He loves my mother's linen sheets and hates his own percale.

He can imitate the sounds of a humpback whale.
I love him not just because I oughter.
But also because blood runs thicker than water.

Growing up in Manhattan, the children good-naturedly conspired to free themselves of their mother's socially correct standards. Caroline, who struggled with weight problems as an adolescent, and John liked to bang around in jeans and tattered sweaters. "She seems to like to look scruffy," a friend told PEOPLE in 1975. "Perhaps it's a reaction to all those clothes her mother buys." Jackie had been named Debutante of the Year 1947; her daughter refused to be paraded as a society trinket.

But if her kids were free spirits, their mother kept them out of the trouble that plagued several cousins. At Jackie's funeral, Senator Ted Kennedy recalled that she had once said, "If you bungle raising your children, nothing much else matters in life." Jackie urged Caroline and John Jr. not to spend too much time with the children of Robert F. Kennedy: RFK Jr. was arrested on a charge of heroin possession but later cleaned up his act, and David died of a cocaine overdose in 1984. Richard Burke, a former aide to Senator Ted Kennedy, told Jerry Oppenheimer in *The Other Mrs. Kennedy*, "With all that stuff going on out at [Ethel Kennedy's Virginia home] Hickory Hill, especially the problems the boys were having, Jackie just didn't want Caroline and John there."

CUB REPORTERS

In their teens and early 20s, both Caroline and John kicked up their heels at New York nightclubs (Studio 54 was a favorite of Caroline's) and had a memorable joint birthday party at New York's Le Club on November 26, 1978, the day between his 18th birthday and her 21st. Their Uncle Ted gave a sad toast: "I shouldn't be doing this tonight," said Senator Kennedy. "By rights, it should have been the father of these two children. Jack loved his children more than anything else. Young John and Caroline bring new life to the family."

■ *Carly Simon sang "Loving You's the Right Thing to Do" at the 1986 wedding reception for Caroline and Edwin Schlossberg (leaving the church, foreground, as John escorted cousin Maria Shriver)*

Later that night, John was involved in a shoving match with some photographers waiting for him outside the restaurant.

After college at Harvard, Caroline, like her father, mother and brother, dabbled in journalism, working for New York's *Daily News* as a copy girl one summer and covering Elvis Presley's funeral for *Rolling Stone*. One day in 1977 at the *Daily News* she had lunch at a neighborhood deli and a UPI photo of her made it back to the office before she did.

■ IN HER FOOTSTEPS ■

Caroline went on to Columbia Law School, also in Manhattan. Recalls Fred Pappert, president of New York's 42nd Street Development Corporation and a friend of Jackie Onassis's for years, "There is a marvelous videotape of Jackie, John and Caroline taken when John graduated from law school and he says, 'I'm happy to be following in my sister's footsteps.'"

It was after her first year of law school that Caroline married author and museum designer Edwin Schlossberg, with her brother serving as best man. (Caroline would return the honor a decade later by serving as matron of honor at John's wedding and hosting a post-honeymoon party at her Park Avenue apartment.) At Caroline's rehearsal dinner, John raised a glass, acknowledging Schlossberg's entry into what had been their special circumscribed world: "It's been the three of us alone for so long. And now we've got a fourth." As the newlyweds stepped into a silver limousine, John blew a kiss to them.

But even that joyous date, July 19, 1986, was fraught with tragedy: it was the 17th anniversary of the day news came that Ted Kennedy's assistant, Mary Jo Kopechne, had drowned in the car accident at Chappaquiddick. On that date in 1999, the Kennedy family would resignedly lower the flag at its Hyannis Port compound to half-staff in memory of John Kennedy Jr.

Though she passed the bar exam on her first try, Caroline has never practiced law, but has co-authored two books, on privacy rights and the Bill of Rights, while raising three children. "Caroline has always been very private and shy," says restaurateur Anne Vanderhoop, who chatted with many a Kennedy at her two eateries on Martha's Vineyard. "Not like John. He's straight out there and forward, not shy at all. They were close in a way. But she's a mom and a housewife and he was a businessman."

■ In Touch 'Til the End ■

Jackie's cousin John H. Davis described Caroline as "happy with her totally isolated life. I know it from the fact she told my mother several years ago, 'I will be perfectly happy to spend all my days in my apartment writing, and playing with my children and looking

"The library is her baby," says author and acquaintance A. E. Hotchner of Caroline (with John at the Kennedy Presidential Library to observe what would have been their father's 80th birthday in 1997).

after my husband.'" Caroline would allow no questions about her family during interviews to promote her books, while her brother tried his best to deal with the avalanche of questions about his family, most notably on May 20, 1994, when he stepped from his mother's Fifth Avenue apartment building to tell reporters that his mother had passed away. Caroline, who like John was at her mother's side when she died, kept her thoughts to herself. And while John introduced his Uncle Ted at the 1988 Democratic Convention, she declined to serve as convention chairwoman four years later.

One of Caroline's few public roles today is as president of the John F. Kennedy Library and Museum in Boston, where in 1989 the library's foundation inaugurated the annual Profile in Courage Award in memory of her late father's Pulitzer Prize–winning book. "They both had their roles to play," said Jeff West, executive director of The Sixth Floor Museum, which occupies the space where Lee Harvey Oswald fired on the president in Dallas. "His role was more social, hers far more strategic. Her role has been more the management of the legacy, the management of the [presidential] library and how the family is perceived."

It was in their father's honor that Caroline and John made what was to be their final public appearance together, in May 1999: to present the Profile in Courage Award at the JFK Library to Sens. John McCain and Russell Feingold for their efforts to reform political campaign financing.

Today it is Caroline, the last survivor of her nuclear family, who must be a model of courage. She will not lack fond memories. John and Caroline spoke on the phone almost daily, including a conversation of nearly half an hour on the day he died, says her housekeeper, Marta Sgubin. The siblings "always smiled when they spoke to each other," agrees Marisa May, co-owner of New York's San Domenico restaurant, where brother and sister shared many a meal. "They seemed like a happy brother and sister. You could tell she was very protective of him. They would spend hours at the table and they would laugh a lot. He would always kiss her when he said goodbye."

CLEARING THE BAR

After John graduated from Brown, he took three years off to travel and to work for nonprofit agencies. He spent the summer of 1983 diving off the coast of New England with underwater explorer Barry Clifford, who would later find the lost 18th century pirate ship *Wydah*. At an October 1983 send-off at Manhattan's Rockabout Disco, John danced with his girlfriend from Brown, Sally Munro; then he headed for London and a party at the American Embassy, attending with his sister. Next came a six-month tour of India. "I know six months isn't a long time," he said, "but I hope to learn as much as I can." A friend said Jackie approved of the journey, having been fascinated by the country when she visited there with President Kennedy in 1962.

A blueblood in blue jeans, John kept a low profile. "You couldn't really have told him apart from all the other backpackers who pass

Kennedy (packing a lawyer's valise on his way to work in 1991) spent four years in the Manhattan District Attorney's office, but "I didn't think he had the passion for prosecution," recalls New York State Supreme Court Judge Richard Lowe.

73

through Delhi," recalls Rajeev Sethi, an artist who hung out with Kennedy in India. "He wore the same grubby jeans and wore his hair long." Vishv Bandhu Gupta, a civil servant who taught Kennedy about India, adds that the unshaven young backpacker stayed in a "dingy hotel" and says with a laugh, "I remember he asked us to promise not to tell his mother how he had been living, as she had obviously wanted him to stay in a private home somewhere. It seemed to me that he had quite a rebellious streak, perhaps against his celebrity back home."

Kennedy ventured into some of the worst slums in the world, eager to confront a way of life beyond his privileged experience. "I remember his mother saying that she hoped his stay in India would give him a chance to come to terms with what life was all about, as his father had done during his wartime service," Sethi says. "I was running a project [for performing artists] at the time in a slum in north Delhi called Shadipur Depot. I asked him if he would be interested in visiting and he leaped at the opportunity. I think it must have been his first experience of really severe urban poverty, but he had a very special kind of receptiveness. His response wasn't at all to cringe away from what he saw, but to dive right in. He wanted to organize English lessons for the children in the slum, and he even gave a few classes, but it was a low-profile project and I was worried that word would get out as to what he was doing and then the whole thing might have turned into a media circus. It was clear that he had been very affected by the experience, but again there was a sense of frustration about wanting to be directly involved rather than just playing the role of an observer. He said, 'I wish I could have been as useful as the experience was useful for me.'"

▪A Star in Search of a Role▪

Returning from India, John got himself an apartment in New York City, on his own there for the first time. In 1984, he accepted a $20,000-a-year job as a management and planning assistant in New York City's Office of Business Development, but as much as he felt

John graduated NYU Law School in 1989. When a reporter asked Jackie for her reaction, she deflected attention to her son, saying, "I want to let the man of the family speak."

drawn to public service, he still had not shaken the allure of the stage. He made his Off-Broadway debut in Brian Friel's play about doomed Irish lovers, *Winners*, in August 1985, cautioning the press, "This is definitely not a professional acting debut by any means. It's just a hobby." Not surprisingly, all six performances at the Irish Arts Center in Manhattan sold out. Everyone entering the theater was searched at the door.

Nye Heron, executive director of the theater, called John "one of the best young actors I've seen in years." Concurred costar and girlfriend Christina Haag, "At one point in rehearsal, we strongly disagreed over the Irish pronunciation of the word God; I was sure I was right and he was sure he was right. But it was confirmed by the director, who was Irish, that John was right. If he had pursued a career as an actor, he would have had a lot of opportunities." In 1988, John shot a two-line cameo in a film made by some Brown friends, *A Matter of Degrees*. But Jackie reportedly discouraged any thought of an acting career. A Brown classmate told Christopher Andersen in *Jackie After Jack*, "She told John in no uncertain terms that acting was beneath him, that he was his father's son and that he had a tradition of public service to uphold." Kennedy told Alan Rothenberg, his supervisor at the L.A. law firm where he was a summer intern in 1988, that he was interested in acting but "it was not something his mother endorsed." After his uncle, actor Peter Lawford, died in December of 1984, no one was left in the family to support a career in the footlights for John.

▪THE SECRETARIES' FAVORITE▪

"Now I can die a happy woman," Jackie joked when John finally decided to attend law school. Like Caroline, who had chosen New York City's Columbia University, he stayed close to his mother, entering New York University's law school in September 1986. John managed to get himself into a legal scrape while a law student: the landlord of his West 86th Street co-op charged in '87 that John had left the two-bedroom apartment in "obnoxious condition," including a two-year layer of dirt and holes in the walls. Kennedy's lawyers paid the landlord an undisclosed financial settlement.

After two years of law school, Kennedy in 1988 gave his galvanizing speech at the Democratic National Convention in Atlanta "I think he'll be involved in public affairs one way or the other in the future, not necessarily running for office," Ted Kennedy said at the time. Meanwhile, Kennedy was taking his only turn as a high-powered corporate legal intern, in an $1,100 a week summer job at Manatt, Phelps, Rothenberg & Phillips, a leading showbiz law firm in Los Angeles with clients such as Prince, Barbra Streisand and Princess Stephanie. Kennedy "just wanted to be one of the guys," recalls his supervisor at the law firm, Alan Rothenberg, citing the time Kennedy joined a number of colleagues to watch a closed-circuit boxing match between Mike Tyson and Michael Spinks in Santa Monica. Everyone

Kennedy was besieged by journalists on his first day of work at the District Attorney's office in 1989. His officemate Owen Carragher later said, "I had this notion that it was going to be a circus. But it didn't take long for all of that to go away."

put a dollar into a pool and drew a random number to bet on which round would decide the bout. Kennedy drew the number 1. Obligingly, Iron Mike dispatched Spinks with one of his trademark upper cuts in the opening round. "John laughed when we all joked, 'Oh, well, the rich get richer,'" says Rothenberg.

Kennedy made a new set of fans in the office that summer. "I test the goodness of people in terms of how they treat people low on the pecking order," Rothenberg says. "And the office services people, messengers and secretaries adored him because he was just so nice to them."

"What really struck me was his restlessness," a lawyer who studied for the bar exam with Kennedy (two-wheel commuting in 1991) told PEOPLE in 1990. "He couldn't sit still for more than ten minutes at a time."

Still, some adjustments had to be made: "We were besieged by calls," from female admirers, Rothenberg says. "We wanted to screen those for him, so we put in a second phone with his own private number."

▪ MOO SHOO MADNESS ▪

John graduated from law school on May 19, 1989, with his sister, mother and Christina Haag attending the Madison Square Garden ceremony. He took the New York State bar exam in July—and flunked. Many law school grads fail the tough New York State test on the first try—over 2,000 of the 6,853 people who took the exam that year did not pass. The setback didn't stop Kennedy from beginning work in August as an assistant district attorney in Manhattan. It was the same office that his cousin Robert F. Kennedy Jr. had served a few years earlier (Bobby Jr. too had failed the bar, but passed on his second try).

Impeccable in suit and tie, Kennedy would clamber on his mountain bike at his apartment on Manhattan's Upper West Side and pedal downtown to the D.A.'s office on Hogan Place, arriving astonishingly crisp and unsmudged. Reporters would be waiting for him. His first afternoon on the job, *New York Post* court reporter Mike Pearl called former counsel to the Manhattan D.A. Paul Shechtman and asked what Kennedy had had for lunch that day at a Chinese restaurant. Shechtman wouldn't say. "The next day I read in the *Post* that John F. Kennedy Jr. had moo shoo pork for lunch," Shechtman told *New York*. "I called Mike and said, 'Why did you write moo shoo pork?' And Mike's response was, 'That's what I would've had for lunch.' It gave me in one short day some sense of what it must be like to be John F. Kennedy Jr."

Michael Cherkasky, former chief of investigations in the D.A.'s office, told *New York* that on that first day, "A paralegal who was making $15,000 a year was offered $10,000 to take a picture of John at his desk."

The fledgling prosecutor paid his dues by handling "intake duty:" interviewing criminal defendants as well as people with complaints to file. "It was funny to see the way they'd react," Cherkasky said. "Having this legend sit down and scribble down your complaint has got to be a little strange." Another former assistant D.A., Jill Konviser, told *New York* the job was hardly Camelot: "You are sitting there interviewing a defendant who is handcuffed to a chair. And it stinks, and people scream at you. We all complained; he never did." As Kennedy's one-time officemate Owen Carragher says, "In ways that are most meaningful, he was just one of us. Except with better-looking girlfriends."

In February 1990, Kennedy took the bar exam again, and waited

DISTRICT ATTORNEY
COUNTY OF NEW YORK
ONE HOGAN PLACE

If Kennedy looked a bit out of sorts as he left the office on May 1, 1990, it was no wonder. That day he had had to tell his boss, Robert Morgenthau, that he had failed the bar exam again. The District Attorney later said, "Some people don't take exams well."

three months to learn that he had finished 11 points shy of a passing grade of 600. On May 1, he trudged up the stone steps to the D.A.'s office, trailing reporters. "I'm very disappointed," he admitted, "but you know, God willing, I'll go back there in July and I'll pass it then. Or I'll pass it when I'm 95. I'm clearly not a major legal genius." Looking back in 1992, he explained to *PrimeTime Live*, "Certainly some of the scrutiny I could do without. When I failed the bar exam [the second time], the *New York Post* had the headline, 'The Hunk Flunks.' "

▪THIRD TIME'S THE CHARM▪

Now his job and chosen profession were at stake. If the hunk flunked a third time, the District Attorney's policy would have required him to resign. "When he failed the second time, I wrote him a note," says former New York City Mayor Ed Koch. The note, Koch says, read, " 'Don't feel badly. I failed the bar exam, too. It didn't stop me and it won't stop you.' He wrote back, 'It's very nice of you to write that,' [but] nevertheless, he [said he] was going to have a much worse summer than he had planned."

The third time, in July of 1990, the charmer prevailed. "We never doubted he would pass," Manhattan D.A. Robert Morgenthau said. To New York State Supreme Court Judge Richard Lowe, who presided over Kennedy's first case, the scion with the famous name was "an average trial attorney. But he handled who he was with extreme grace." By the time he left his post in July 1993, Kennedy would win all six of his decisions at trial. He even won over at least one of the people he put behind bars. "Even though his job was to put me away, I liked the guy," Venard Garvin, whom Kennedy convicted of drug possession in 1992, told *New York*. "At the recess, I spoke to him. I remember I said, 'It's the job—it's not you.' "

In some sense, it *was* him. Judge Lowe recalls the time an elderly German judge and his wife happened to be sitting in the courtroom and he asked Kennedy to step forward and be introduced to them. "The [German] judge and his wife welled up with tears, they were overtaken with emotion because of the impact [President] Kennedy had on the German people," Lowe says. Afterwards, Lowe apologized to Kennedy for putting him on the spot because "I knew he did not wear his Kennedy-ism on his sleeve. He understood. It was just," he adds, "one of those encapsulating moments."

SEXIEST MAN

Son, adventurer, lawyer, editor, husband: John F. Kennedy Jr. was all these things, but perhaps no label stuck to him more securely than that of Sexiest Man Alive, a laurel bestowed on him in PEOPLE's Sept. 12, 1988 cover story. In the three previous Sexiest Man issues (and in every one since), the winner had been a TV or film star. Richard Sanders, then a PEOPLE senior editor on the entertainment beat, says Kennedy out-Hollywooded Hollywood. "That was an especially fallow time in terms of movies and TV stars," Sanders remembers. "It forced the editors to go out of the box. Once they did he was the first guy standing at the door—he just hit everybody in the face."

Kennedy had come into his own in the 1980s, adds Sanders, now Executive Editor of ENTERTAINMENT WEEKLY. "His looks really solidified somewhere between his teen years and his twenties," he

■ *"A lot of people I know ask to be stars and complain about it,"* *says friend Hilary Shepard-Turner of Kennedy (on the Hyannis* *beach in 1980). "He handled it very well for someone who didn't* *ask for it."*

Of PEOPLE's *13 Sexiest Men to date, Kennedy was the best-seller. The 1988 cover story described him as "a friendly, decent, remarkably down-to-earth guy who once followed a stranger down the street to return the five bucks the man had dropped."*

says. "He was kind of gawky and cute as a teenager, but now women were talking about him not just as John-John or as JFK's son but as this guy who was tremendously appealing in his own right. We were just riding that wave."

A tsunami, it seemed. "In the mid-eighties," recalls Kennedy pal Richard Wiese, "John could go around New York City fairly anonymously. But when PEOPLE awarded him that title, there was a big change in media attention." Kennedy, who continued to play football shirtless, toss frisbees and even perform the occasional handstand in Central Park, wore his new crown lightly. "Listen, people can say a lot worse things about you," he told Barbara Walters, "than you are attractive, and you look good in a bathing suit."

His friends, though, didn't let him forget. "We'd tease him about the 'Sexiest Man Alive,'" says Wiese. "We'd say to him, 'Is he the sexiest man—on this earth? Ever? He'd laugh and cuss at you and say, 'You're just jealous.' Among his friends, that was fodder for a lot of jokes. He liked being razzed. He'd rather be the butt of the joke than tell the joke about someone else. It meant someone wasn't kissing his butt."

Poking fun at his own image, John attended one Halloween party as Michelangelo's David and another covered with glitter as the Golden Boy. Hilary Shepard-Turner, a friend of Daryl Hannah's, remembers,

"He had a great sense of humor about himself. We used to make fun of his perfect hair and call him 'Helmet Head.' We once had him paged in an airport, 'Paging Mr. Head, Mr. Helmet Head.' He answered the page. He thought it was hysterical. He always signed his letters H. Head from then on."

PRINCE OF WAILS

Publicist Ken Sunshine recalls that during a 1993 campaign stop at New York City's Zabar's deli for then-Mayor David Dinkins, "A scream came from several old ladies, screaming, 'John! John!' It was like the Beatles. They were buying lox. There was this crush. A cheese display went flying at one point and a big tough cop said, 'It's a lox riot!' And we had to get him out of there. People wanted a piece of him. It was wild." At Gallagher's Steak House in Manhattan, says manager Bryan Reidy, admirers didn't have to fight through any cheese displays. "Women would brush into him at the bar so they could say, 'I touched John!'"

When Kennedy visited former Republican National Committee chairman Haley Barbour, recalled former *George* editor-at-large Tony Blankley, "female staffers were coming up with the lamest excuses, like, 'Just checking the paper clip supply.'"

Whenever he needed a break from lawyering or editing, Kennedy often drew a crowd during his bare-chested antics in Central Park. "When girls started to watch our games," says football pal David Check, "they were watching one guy. I can't blame them. He had a body like Adonis."

Associating with Kennedy had certain upsides. Owen Carragher, who worked with Kennedy in the Manhattan District Attorney's office, remembers quarreling with the office cleaning lady, who subsequently refused to clean his office. But the day after Kennedy set up his desk in the same office, things changed. "I now had the cleanest office in the building," Carragher says, laughing. "When he wasn't there, she wouldn't come. Women responded that way to him all the time."

John and Daryl Hannah were said to be planning a wedding soon after returning from this 1993 holiday in Palau, Micronesia, but Caroline Kennedy Schlossberg chided reporters, "You guys are really far off."

And not just women. "I think John was even more handsome than his father," says former Kennedy administration White House photographer Jacques Lowe. Lawrence Schwartzwald, one of the New York photographers who spent many a day in pursuit of Kennedy, remembers, "John was a movie star without being in the movies. Of all the celebrities that you photograph, to photographers as a whole, male, female, young and old, they all had a crush on John Kennedy. I've seen 60-year-old photographers talk about him, and it was like they were talking about their girlfriends, they were in love with the guy."

▪Passion Flowers▪

Girls had been swooning over JFK Jr. since his schoolboy days. In 1977, when he was a student at Phillips Academy in Andover, Mass., he attended the New York premiere of *Saturday Night Fever* and nearly upstaged the film's star, John Travolta, who was waving to the crowd when a fresh round of delighted squeals made him turn and look over his shoulder. There was Kennedy, getting out of the next limousine.

Jenny Christian, an Andover classmate and daughter of a New York surgeon, became John's first serious girlfriend. Jackie liked her, and Jenny, who was 16 when she and John met in 1976, just after he started 11th grade, became a regular at Hyannis Port and at 1040 Fifth Avenue. They were all but inseparable for three years. She was by his side when he graduated from Andover in 1979, even though by this time she was finishing her first year at Harvard. The core of the attraction was that Jenny liked John for John. "If he had fallen out of a pickup truck he still would have been irresistible to me," Christian later said. "He was extremely handsome, nice and sweet. It was a great romance."

Another early crush was Meg Azzoni, who turned up on his arm at the RFK tennis tournament in Forest Hills, N.Y., in August 1977. John, working as an usher at the tournament, watched the matches with Azzoni from a front-row seat.

When Kennedy began his freshman year at Brown, he'd emerge from his dorm room in the morning to find girls sleeping in the hallway. As an undergraduate, John dated Sally Munro, who had graduated from the same girls' prep school, Concord Academy in Massachusetts, as Caroline and bore a strong physical resemblance to her. The pair dated from around 1981 to 1985, enjoying frequent bike rides together. Munro, who had grown up in a $5-million home in Marblehead, Mass., a town where her family had lived for generations, would graduate Brown in 1982, a year before he did.

While dating Munro, John shared an off-campus house in Providence with Christiane Amanpour—now a celebrated foreign correspondent for CNN—and Christina Haag, the daughter of a marketing executive and a graduate of Manhattan's exclusive Brearley School. Haag and JFK had been friends since they were teenagers. Four years later, both now living in New York City—she a student of drama at Juilliard, he a management and planning assistant in New York City's Office of Business Development—they connected on a romantic level when they costarred in the Off-Broadway play *Winners* in 1985.

House-sharing again, Haag and Kennedy spent the summer of 1988 in Venice, Calif., she appearing in a play in Hollywood's Tiffany

Kennedy and Hannah (in New York City in 1994) often cuddled in public. One neighbor told PEOPLE *in 1993 she saw them dancing on a rooftop. "Even if you didn't know who they were, you'd be entranced."*

Theater. One friend said at the time, "They bring out the best in each other." But they split in 1991. Mrs. Onassis remained so fond of Haag that she paid a condolence call when Haag's father died in 1992.

■MADONNA AND THE MODELS■

In the late 1980s and early 1990s, Kennedy's increasing celebrity began to attract women who were celebrities themselves. He and

Madonna dated a few times, and jogged together in Central Park. When John took her to meet his mother, Jackie "hit the roof," viewing the Material Girl as a "crass social climber," according to a friend of John's who told the story to biographer Christopher Andersen. By arriving separately at plays, parties and dinners, Kennedy and Madonna largely managed to conceal their relationship from the press. But Andersen reported that Madonna's divorce from hothead actor Sean Penn was not yet complete, and Penn was seething. When Kennedy tried to introduce himself at a party, Penn told him, "I know who you are. You owe me an apology." Madonna jokingly sent Kennedy a funeral wreath the next morning with a card inscribed, "My deepest sympathy." Years later, Madonna would agree to write a column for the premiere issue of *George*—about what she would do if she were President.

Sarah Jessica Parker canoodled with Kennedy for a spell in 1991, and quipped, "It's unfair, as a woman, to have to stand next to him." A Brazilian TV star named Xuxa reportedly spied a photograph of JFK in a magazine, "thought he was a model" and sent him a photo of herself with accompanying video. Ever gallant, John asked her out.

Xuxa had it almost right: John wasn't a model, but he dated them: Wilhelmina's Julie Baker; Ashley Richardson, SPORTS ILLUSTRATED swimsuit issue cover girl; and Click's Audra Avizienis, who said, "He has this quiet sadness. There's something pensive and sad about him."

▪ HANNAH AND HER MISTER ▪

The one celebrity Kennedy dated seriously was an actress he had met when both were 18. John, his mother and Jenny Christian were vacationing in St. Martin when he met a slender young actress named Daryl Hannah at the La Samanna resort.

Hannah, a Chicago native who had just made her film debut in *The Fury*, had been hard hit by her parents' divorce when she was seven—she had suffered visions of witches and leprechauns at the time—and she still had some quirks even though her mother Sue

Ferris, a descendant of the inventor of the Ferris wheel, had remarried billionaire Chicago real estate developer Jerrold Wexler, whose brother Haskell is an accomplished Hollywood cinematographer. Kennedy and Christian used to joke about Hannah's habit of lugging around a teddy bear at La Sammana.

Kennedy ran into Hannah again in 1988, at the September wedding of John's aunt, Lee Radziwill, to Herb Ross, who was directing Hannah in *Steel Magnolias*. Later that year, on October 4, New York City newspapers breathlessly noted what may have been the couple's first date in Manhattan: Kennedy took Hannah to a West Village club, then a bar called Automatic Slim's, and wound up the evening at a TriBeCa club called S.T.P., where John and Daryl shot pool and listened to the Dennis B. Harvey Band and High Ground until the joint closed in the wee hours. The following Memorial Day—although he was still dating Haag—John took Daryl cruising on Virginia's Smith Mountain Lake on a 46-foot yacht. When Hannah became ill while filming *At Play in the Fields of the Lord* in the Brazilian jungle, Kennedy sent her 1,000 red roses.

Though the actress and the hunk were growing closer, Hannah was still embroiled in a stormy relationship with "Running on Empty" singer Jackson Browne, with whom she lived in Santa Monica, Calif. In 1992 police were called to their home after a domestic quarrel that resulted, friends told PEOPLE, in Hannah suffering bruises and a broken finger. No police report was filed against Browne, who denied any wrong-doing, saying, "It was untrue that I was violent. We had been breaking up for quite a while. Absolutely no assault occurred."

By 1993, Kennedy and Hannah were inseparable. They attended John's 10-year reunion at Brown and for a time lived together in Hannah's apartment on the Upper West Side of Manhattan. In September 1993 press reports floated the notion that the pair were about to wed. But John had been dealt a willowy wild card: in November, *Newsday* reported that "the word around town is that the woman with whom Kennedy has been spending so much time is Calvin Klein's director of public relations, Carolyn Bessette."

Kennedy pal John Perry Barlow recalled that autumn, when Kennedy began to talk about Bessette. "He wasn't going to pursue it because he was loyal to Daryl," Barlow, the former Grateful Dead lyricist, told *New York*. "And he maintained a platonic relationship with her until after he and Daryl had broken up."

The end for John and Daryl came shortly after Jackie died. In early 1994, as Mrs. Onassis struggled with cancer, Kennedy and Hannah took a break in the Cayman Islands. They were still very close when Jackie died in May. But although Hannah attended the funeral, she was left behind when the family attended the burial at Arlington National Cemetery. By August, after five and half years together, she and John had broken up. Some close to the family believed Mrs. Onassis looked down on Hollywood—"Jackie never came out and said so, but you got the feeling that she didn't approve of his relationship with Daryl and all that it implied," a friend of John's told PEOPLE in 1995. Yet Hannah's mother insisted there was never any tension, telling *The Chicago Sun-Times*, "Daryl told me [Onassis] has been very warm and affectionate." A friend of Daryl's wondered if the breakup resulted because "it was as if he felt he needed to carry the Kennedy torch with dignity, and Daryl didn't fit in." But Kennedy himself once implied that Hannah's background had nothing to do with it. Chris Cuomo (whose brother Andrew married John's cousin Kerry) recalled Kennedy saying that "he had played the field for a long time and worried about never meeting anyone, and then one day he met Carolyn and from the first minute he knew that she'd be the one."

10

HIS OWN MAN

On the morning of May 20, 1994, a somber-faced John Kennedy stood beneath the awning of the entrance to Jacqueline Kennedy Onassis's apartment building at 1040 Fifth Avenue and told a group of reporters, "Last night at around 10:15 my mother passed on. She was surrounded by her friends and her family and her books and the people and the things that she loved." Hands in his pockets, his expression somber, Kennedy quietly continued, "She did it in her own way and in her own terms, and we all feel lucky for that and now she's in God's hands."

With the passing of the woman who introduced herself to her son's friends, "Hi, I'm John's mother," Kennedy was finally ready, at 33, to begin doing things in his own way—and on his own terms.

Ironically for a man who had spent much of his adult life eluding packs of bothersome paparazzi, Kennedy chose to join the Fourth

■ *When Kennedy (with Jackie in 1986) lost his mother in 1994, remembers pal Richard Wiese, "He said it was a clarifying moment [because it showed him that] a lot of little stuff didn't matter and what did matter was family."*

Estate. In tandem with Michael J. Berman, an old chum from his undergraduate days at Brown, he set out to launch *George*, cheekily named after the country's first President, aimed not at the Washington intelligentsia, but rather at the broad, apolitical masses. In a market saturated with glossies, where 90 percent of all start-ups fold, it was hardly an easy sell. Despite repeated petitions, several U.S. publishers turned Kennedy and Berman down.

⬛JOINING THE OTHER SIDE⬛

Even Kennedy's own family was less than thrilled with the idea, though it seemed a quirky tribute to both the journalism and editing past of his mother and the political legacy of his father. "When he first wanted to start the magazine, he said his family really didn't want him to do it," says Keith Stein, a Toronto businessman who was helping line up new investors in *George* at the time of Kennedy's death. "He said they said it was like he was joining 'the other side.'"

Eventually, Kennedy and Berman secured some $20 million in backing from the French publishing empire Hachette-Filipacchi. Operating as what Kennedy described as "a bubble gum and shoestring operation," the two friends hunkered down in a midtown Manhattan office building and began the laborious task of creating their dream magazine. From the start, Kennedy explained, the idea was to treat politicians as celebrities and to "talk about politics with the same sort of informed casualness [people] talk about the new movie coming out or a new record."

The Kennedy name was magnetic: 175 advertisers signed on for the first issue, which enjoyed a robust press run of 500,000 copies and hit newsstands in September with the resounding thump of its 280 pages. But most eyes, inevitably, were on Kennedy. At a press conference to introduce the glossy bimonthly, Kennedy mingled easily with reporters, quipping, "I don't think that I have seen as many of you in one place since they announced the results of my first bar exam."

With an estimated personal fortune of as much as $74 million, Kennedy could have merely lent his name and handsome face to the endeavor and called it a day. But he seemed determined to prove wrong the media doomsayers who predicted a quick demise for the insouciant concoction. A backpack slung across his shoulder, he boarded his bike or a subway each day and rode to his modestly appointed office with its spectacular view of New York Harbor.

Involving himself in all aspects of the magazine, from devising story ideas, meeting production schedules and editing copy to writing headlines, coverlines and his own editor's note, Kennedy often worked late into the night and on weekends. He could cajole celebrated names to contribute, and pulled the best from those around him. "He helped me enormously to find my own voice," says Paul Begala, a contributing editor and former presidential adviser to Bill Clinton. "He would goad me and prod me."

To promote the new magazine, Kennedy was willing to give up some of his coveted privacy. He made a cameo appearance on *Murphy Brown*, allowed the ever-present paparazzi to get closer and posed for pictures in almost every issue. The one thing he wouldn't tolerate was tabloid chatter; all staffers were required to sign a confidentiality agreement barring them from speaking or writing about Kennedy while employed at the magazine, or even after they left.

By mid-1998, with the magazine on fairly stable footing, Kennedy was able to boast with a broad smile that during the secretive development of *George*, "Everyone was like, 'What's John doing with his time?' Now here it is, two and a half years [later]. It's pretty cool."

Kennedy found it satisfying to hold out the microphone for once, and he made it clear he would do it in his own way. "It's not my nature to be inquisitorial," he explained. "I think it is my nature to be curious." That curiosity led him to interview an eclectic crop of public figures, among them Nation of Islam leader Louis Farrakhan, evangelist Billy Graham, George Wallace and Secretary of State Madeleine Albright, who recalled, "he was a sophisticated questioner and a very warm human being."

As the years went by and the initial excitement surrounding *George* waned, Kennedy's attention began to drift. "In the early days, John had his hands on everything. He wanted to do everything," recalls former *George* copy editor Don Armstrong. "But after a couple of years, he got a little tired of it and started focusing on different issues."

What rarely flagged, however, was his graciousness and approachability. "One night we were on deadline and he just showed up with five pizzas," says Smith Galtney, who was a researcher at the magazine. "It was raining out and he was soaked, but we were all hungry and he'd gone out on his bike to bring us the pizza."

If his quick temper was known to flare from time to time—he and Berman nearly came to blows in the hallway; Berman later departed the magazine—his graceful manners were also on constant display. His thank-you notes were prized by the magazine's contributors. Staffers were routinely rewarded with his own courtside Knicks season tickets, and during the 1996 World Series, he procured seats for the entire staff for Game One of the Yankees-Braves face-off. When employees would bring their kids to the office, he'd invite the tots to make prank calls all over the world. "He was like a guy in a fraternity who seemed like he was around old pals," says Armstrong. "He was oblivious to his celebrity."

For all of *George's* quirky appeal, there was never any doubt that Kennedy's glamor was indispensable to its survival. "Of course, he knew it was his name that kept the magazine alive," says his uncle Jamie Auchincloss. "If he didn't know that, he shouldn't be where he was." And even as the magazine sunk deeper into the red, he never lost his sense of humor. "I mean, we're like the Conan O'Brien of magazines," Kennedy joked in March, 1999. "You know, we're still here."

True—but at a cost. Though *George* is the largest political magazine in the country, with a paid circulation of 405,894, it reportedly bleeds some $4 million in losses annually. The 1997 split between Kennedy and Berman, whose office screaming matches were legendary, fueled rumors that the magazine was about to be sold. Shortly after Kennedy's death, Jack Kliger, president of Hachette-Filipacchi Mag-

After his mother's funeral in May 1994, Kennedy began to come into his own. "My mother was very strict with me when I was a child," he once told an acquaintance.

azines, told *The New York Times* that there had never been "a cohesive marketing strategy stated beyond the personal dynamism of John," and announced that the magazine's future would soon be discussed with the trustees of Kennedy's estate.

Within the clan, support for Kennedy's effort remained weak at best. In a 1997 essay, he rankled two of his cousins—Joseph, the

Always at home on the streets of New York, Kennedy entertained an exuberant group of children in 1985 at a roller skating party in Brooklyn to benefit the underprivileged.

Massachussetts representative derided for annulling his 12-year marriage which had produced twin boys, and Michael, accused of sleeping with an underage babysitter (and just months later killed in a ski accident)—by calling them "poster boys for bad behavior." He chastised, "To whom much is given, much is expected, right?" Complicating the broadside, Kennedy included a seminude picture of himself in the issue.

The only family support Kennedy seemed confident of was that of his mother. "She had a good sense of humor and I don't think she was a slave to conventional wisdom," he told Larry King at the time of the magazine's launch, 16 months after Jackie's death. "I think that there is a certain irony in the whole enterprise and I think she would have appreciated it."

▪ IN THE COCKPIT AT LAST ▪

Another of Kennedy's post-Jackie passions would not have pleased his mother nearly as much: flying. His interest in aviation was evident from his earliest years in the White House. If the President refused him a helicopter ride, young John would burst into tears. "So, he got to go on a lot of helicopter trips," smiles his uncle, Jamie Auchincloss. "He had his father wrapped around his finger."

His mother was a different story. "He told me that he wanted to fly from the time he was a little boy, but that his mother was against him taking flying lessons," recalls Lois Cappelen, a waitress at C.J. Cannon's, a family-style restaurant near Flight Safety International, the highly-regarded Florida flight school in Vero Beach, along the Atlantic coast, where Kennedy would earn his wings in April 1998. "After his mother died, he decided he would fulfill his dream and get his license."

He had flirted with that dream years earlier, before his mother's fears grounded him. Flight instructor Arthur Marx first gave Kennedy flying lessons while he was still an undergraduate at Brown. "When he wasn't working, he wanted to be flying," says Marx. "He really dug it." CNN's Christiane Amanpour, a close friend who shared an off-campus house with Kennedy during his Brown years, also remembers those lessons. "It's been a passion for as long as I have known him," she reported on her network after his death.

Kennedy's first flying contraption was a $13,000 Falcon 582— a single-seat powered parachute, purchased from Buckeye Industries Inc. of Argos, Indiana. To train Kennedy to fly the craft, which does not require a pilot's license, Lloyd Howard, a Buckeye vice president and design engineer, traveled to Albany, New York, in August 1996. "We wanted to make sure that he knew how to operate the plane," says Howard. After two hours of training, Kennedy took off—and didn't return for almost an hour. "We could not get him to come down," says Howard. "He just loved to fly."

A little over a year later, Kennedy traded his single-seater for a $14,300 two-seat Buckeye, the craft he was flying last Memorial Day weekend when he landed bumpily, breaking his left ankle. At the time of his death, he was thinking of upgrading his powered parachute yet again. "I'll be at the big air show in Oshkosh this August," he'd recently e-mailed Howard. "I'd love to check out your new Millennium 2000 model."

"John was a good pilot," Howard asserts. "He was very easy to train and a very conscious pilot. If John had any idea that he was going to get into fog or in a position that he would not have been able to handle, he would not have taken off. John was an adventurer, not a daredevil."

After Kennedy's death, there would be debate not only about his fitness to fly, but also about whether his wife, Carolyn, wanted to be skybound with him at the controls. Howard maintains that Carolyn had herself been bitten with the aviation bug, and was planning to learn to fly a powered parachute. Ethan Bagg, a charter pilot who often flew the Kennedys to and from Martha's Vineyard, says that Carolyn loved to fly, usually relaxing with a book on his charter flights. "She was happy to fly with John," he says.

Kennedy offered conflicting statements about his wife's enthusiasm for flying with him in the cockpit. Last year, he told *USA Today*, "The only person I've been able to get to go up with me—who looks forward to it as much as I do—is my wife." But the week before the crash, he told Jackie biographer C. David Heymann, "Nobody likes flying with me, including my wife. I'm no Charles Lindbergh."

Such self-effacement was characteristic. "He loved flying," says

Willing to sacrifice some privacy to promote his new venture, Kennedy made a cameo as himself on Murphy Brown, *starring Candice Bergen, in September 1995, the month* George *hit newsstands.*

Marx. He was attracted not only by the freedom and independence it symbolized, but the camaraderie it afforded. Initially he operated out of New Jersey's Teterboro airport, whose celebrity high-fliers include Bill Cosby, Harrison Ford and John Travolta. But he switched his base of operations to nearby Essex airport because he preferred the laid-back atmosphere. "He was just one of the guys," says Larry Lorenzo, owner of the Caldwell Flight Academy. "He'd hang out like everybody else and talk about flying."

Rapidly, Kennedy graduated from the two-seat powered parachute to a Cessna 182 and then to a more powerful and sophisticated single-engine, six-seat Piper Saratoga II that he'd bought second-hand for about $300,000 and planned to fly to his cousin Rory's wed-

Kennedy (checking out a plane) "always asked me about flying,"
says Jerry Wiener, a pilot and flight instructor on Martha's Vineyard.
"By getting his own license, he could get where he needed to go, have
more privacy and not have all that contact."

ding. He also liked to spend weekends buzzing over the Cape Cod
coastline near the family home in Gay Head in the two-cylinder
ultralight plane that he purchased two years ago. "By getting his own
license, he could get where he needed to go, have more privacy,"
says Jerry Wiener, a flight instructor on the Cape who can still
remember the sight of Kennedy as a gap-toothed boy, running
around with a toy helicopter in his hand.

With about 300 logged hours under his belt, Kennedy was confident—but not cocky. "If anything," says flight instructor Marx,
who spent about 15 hours aloft with Kennedy, "he handled the
airplane better than he thought he did." Moreover, attests charter

pilot Ethan Bagg, who often, at Kennedy's behest, flew the amateur pilot from the Essex airport to Martha's Vineyard when weather conditions were dicey: "He was smart enough to know his limitations."

After years of struggling to carve a place for himself in the world, Kennedy seemed finally to be gaining a sense of balance. Asked by a caller on a phone-in TV show, "What aspect of your personality do you credit your mother the most for having instilled in you?" he answered, "I think that there is a sense of not worrying too much about things that you can't control, and living your life."

LOVE AT LAST

11

The romantic version goes like this: at a fateful bash in 1993, John Kennedy was introduced to Carolyn Bessette, a tall, slender, blonde beauty with elegance, style and a spontaneous sense of humor. "It was love at first sight," says Paul Wilmot, a former boss of Bessette's at Calvin Klein, where she worked for the designer as a publicist. "They never saw anybody else again."

A more mundane version has it that Kennedy and Bessette actually first met in 1992 when America's Most Eligible Bachelor was still linked to Daryl Hannah. Struck by the figure Bessette cut as she jogged through Central Park, he engaged her in conversation. A few days later, he appeared at Calvin Klein and, guided by her tasteful fashion instincts, purchased three suits. "He maintained a platonic relationship with her until after he and Daryl had broken up," his friend John Perry Barlow told *New York* magazine.

Either way, it was clear: in Bessette, Kennedy had finally found

■ *In a secret ceremony attended by 40 intimates, Kennedy wed Carolyn Bessette on September 21, 1996. "Everyone knew he had probably found his true soulmate," says her friend Paul Wilmot.*

■ *John and Carolyn revelled in their new love in 1996. Four days before he died, at the meeting Kennedy had with Toronto businessman Keith Stein, "he talked about having kids as if it was imminent in their future," Stein says. "He mentioned his wife a lot. She was a real reference point. It was clear they had a very strong relationship."*

his match. "John was intrigued by Carolyn because she was challenging," says pal Richard Wiese. Five years younger than Kennedy, she could alternately ignite a dinner party with her smile and warmth, or frost reporters with her glower. "She was a tough-minded individual who knew what she wanted," says

Jackie biographer C. David Heymann. "She was not a woman like a lot of the women he'd gone with in the past, who had bowed down to him."

▪SHADES OF JACKIE▪

"There was a striking similarity between Carolyn and John's mother," says historian Barbara Kellerman, who has written extensively on the presidency. "Good-looking, slender, fashionable—even the lyrical French last name." JFK Jr. biographer Wendy Leigh was struck by Bessette's "tremendous elegance combined with an unusual sex appeal" and her ability to be "very clever with the media, by turns reclusive and not so reclusive." Others noted that, like Jackie, Bessette was athletic, Roman Catholic and had come from a broken home.

Bessette's ready-for-prime-time elegance was honed in manicured Greenwich, Conn., where she grew up with her mother, Ann, a public school teacher and administrator, her twin older sisters, Lauren and Lisa, and her stepfather, orthopedic surgeon Richard Freeman. (Her father, William Bessette, who was divorced from her mother when Carolyn was eight and with whom she had little contact, sells cabinets in New Rochelle, N.Y.) Voted "Ultimate Beautiful Person" while a senior at St. Mary's High School, she was the only one, recalled former classmate Claudia Slocum, "who could pull off wearing the ill-fitting school uniform pants."

While earning an education degree from Boston University, Bessette was featured on the cover of "B.U.'s Most Beautiful Women" calendar. She sat for a few more photographers but apparently was not interested in pursuing a modeling career. "She couldn't sit still long enough," a photographer told the *New York Post* in 1996. "I think she's so smart, she wanted a better job."

Teaching did not seem the ticket, either, despite her degree. "At the time, I felt a little underdeveloped myself to be completely responsible for 25 other people's children," she was quoted as saying in 1992. "And to a large extent, I felt it wouldn't be provocative enough for me."

Soon after graduating in 1988, Bessette took a job as a saleswoman at the Calvin Klein store in Boston's Chestnut Hill Mall. Within a year, she earned herself a ticket to the designer's Manhattan head-quarters to handle such celebrity clients as Annette Bening, Faye Dunaway and Diane Sawyer.

By the time she crossed Kennedy's path, Bessette had slimmed to a size 6, lightened her pale brown hair to a honey blond and had dealt with her share of celebrity beaus, among them Calvin Klein model Michael Bergin, John Cullen, who plays hockey with the Tampa Bay Lightning, and Alessandro Benetton of the Italian fashion company. She was successful in her own right, pulling down a six-figure salary. "She was magic and everyone in the business loved her," says Wilmot. "She was so diplomatically gifted."

And attractive. A slinky 5'10", with alabaster skin and aquamarine eyes, Bessette had long since developed unerring confidence in her own sense of style. Her look was casual, nonchalant, her hair often pulled back in a ponytail, her only jewelry a gold cross. "She was effortlessly beautiful," says Jonathan Soroff, who became a close friend when Bessette worked briefly as a nightclub promoter in Boston in the late 1980s. "She was very understated, very classic, very monochromatic."

▪ON THE SIDEWALKS OF NEW YORK▪

From the start of the Bessette-Kennedy courtship in 1993, photographers could not get enough of America's prettiest couple. Smooching in Central Park—click—hugging in Milan—click—goofing around in Paris—click—cuddling on the streets of TriBeCa, the trendy downtown section of Manhattan where they set up house in a roomy loft in 1995. Click, click, click.

Rumors of an impending split were ignited in February 1996, when an amateur photographer videotaped the duo in a lovers' spat in Washington Square Park. The tape showed Bessette and

"When she was dating John [the couple strolled in Washington, D.C. in April 1996], she'd say, 'You always need to be careful what you say. No matter where I go, somehow it will be on the front page,'" says pal Dana Gallo Strayton.

Kennedy shoving each other, then Kennedy removing a ring from her finger. When he tried to grab Friday, the black and white mutt they owned together, she yelled, "You've got my ring. You're not getting my dog!"

After she stormed off, Kennedy sat down on a curb and buried his head in his hands. Moments later, the two made up. But the excerpts that were played over and over on TV news and entertainment shows did not include the reconciliation.

That June, Bessette seemed to disappear, reviving rumors of a breakup. In fact, by then Bessette had quit her job and the pair was engaged, a decision that had not come easily to Bessette.

The 1998 completion of renovations to Manhattan's Grand Central Station—a project that had been important to Jackie—coaxed Caroline and her husband Edwin Schlossberg to join John and Carolyn at the gala.

While she was considering Kennedy's proposal, says Dana Gallo Strayton, 34, one of Bessette's Boston University roommates, "She was excited but she wanted to make sure it was the right decision. She knew the limelight would be there." Amazingly, news of the engagement did not leak until two days after Kennedy, 35, and Bessette, 30, had sprung their greatest surprise on the public: *fait accompli* nuptials.

200 WILD HORSES, 40 WEDDING GUESTS

Six months in the planning, the clandestine wedding took place before 40 close friends and relatives in a ramshackle chapel on

Georgia's Cumberland Island on Saturday, September 21, 1996. The planning, which depended on the discretion of devoted friends, "required the skill of a James Bond and the whole CIA," said Letitia Baldrige, who was White House chief of staff for Jackie Kennedy.

The festivities began Friday evening at Greyfield Inn, a nine-bedroom mansion on Cumberland Island, a sparsely populated, 18-mile strip of sand a mile off the south Georgia coast where some 200 wild horses roam free. Kennedy had raised no suspicions back in Manhattan when he'd slipped from his office at *George* by slinging a golf bag over his shoulder and announcing he was off for a holiday. That weekend he toasted Bessette for having made him "the happiest man alive."

On Saturday evening, the ceremony took place in the tiny, wood-frame First African Baptist Church, built in 1893 by former slaves. Among the elite packing the chapel's eight wooden pews were *paterfamilias* Ted Kennedy and his wife, Vicki; Jackie's sister Lee Radziwill Ross and her son Anthony Radziwill, who was best man; and Jackie's longtime companion, financier Maurice Tempelsman. Caroline Kennedy Schlossberg was matron of honor, her daughters, Rose, 8, and Tatiana, 6, were flower girls, and her youngest, Jack, 3, was ring-bearer.

In the chapel, illuminated only by candles and kerosene lamps, all eyes were on Bessette. She'd spent three months working with her friend Narciso Rodriguez of Nino Cerruti to design her $40,000 gown, of pearl white floor-length silk crepe, with a hand-rolled tulle silk veil. She walked down the aisle clutching a simple bouquet of lilies of the valley in hands covered by long silk gloves. Breaking the spell, little Jack gazed up and asked loudly, "Why is Carolyn all dressed up?"

Following a brief Catholic service, the guests returned to Greyfield, where they dined on shrimp, swordfish and a three-tier wedding cake iced with vanilla butter cream frosting. After dinner the newlyweds danced to Prince's "Forever in My Life." By the time the press caught on and trundled to Cumberland, Kennedy and Bessette had gotten a running start on their honeymoon in Turkey and Greece.

▪FROSTY SMILES▪

Two weeks later, the newlyweds were met by a torrent of flashes as they emerged from their TriBeCa building. "This is a big change for anyone, and for a private citizen even more so," Kennedy told the media throng. "I ask that you give Carolyn all the privacy and room you can."

Right.

The new Mrs. Kennedy was now among the most watched Americans in the world. *New York Times* columnist Maureen Dowd dubbed her "Our New Obsession." Fashion designers salivated, sensing in her a Diana-esque mannequin upon which to drape their wares. Explained designer John Bartlett, "She's very bohemian but also very glamorous. She loves to mix things. She doesn't play by anybody's rules." Liz Tilberis of *Harper's Bazaar* said, "We'd love to have her on the cover. She's going to be an amazing symbol of American style."

Gripping her husband's arm, the new Mrs. Kennedy bore up admirably at public functions, freezing a smile for the cameras. But the constant attention quickly took its toll. "She was a fun-loving girl at the beginning," says Kennedy biographer Leigh. "She went into a kind of shell. She was very frosty at public occasions. She was not accessible—nor could she have been." Says pal Wilmot, "She didn't complain. She didn't talk about it because everybody else did."

The first wave of rumors had it that Bessette was pregnant; the next insisted that she and Kennedy were splitting up. Bubby's restaurant in TriBeCa, one of John and Carolyn's favorite breakfast hangouts, became a refuge for Bessette when the break-up rumors became shrill. "She would have to hide in here. She'd go out the back door to get out," says Seth Price, who co-owns the eatery. "It was just horrible. She just wanted to spend time with her husband."

President Clinton, who was inspired as a boy by his handshake with President Kennedy, took particular pleasure in showing the junior Kennedy and his wife through the White House in March 1998.

Nothing angered the gentlemanly Kennedy more than when the press criticized his wife. "People wrote he was stupid, he failed the bar, his magazine was no good—it never bothered him," says one close friend. "But when people would take out after Carolyn, it would just set him off. He said, 'Look, I put myself out there, but she never did. She never called a press conference, never gave a speech.' That used to really just infuriate him."

The unwanted publicity took another toll. Both Bessette and Kennedy, it was reported, wanted children—a son called Flynn, if the father had his wish. But, their friend Christa D'Souza told London's *Daily Telegraph*, "they were holding back because neither of them could bear the idea of all the media attention." Indeed, that had been Bessette's foremost concern when considering whether to marry Kennedy. "She said to me, 'What will it be like with the children? We'll always be hounded,'" says roommate Strayton. More

113

Frequently spotted on the streets of TriBeCa with his dog Friday (together, in March 1997), Kennedy tried to be a regular guy. "I grew up most of my life in very ordinary circumstances," he said in 1995.

recently, says Toronto businessman Keith Stein, Kennedy "told me they might leave New York when they had kids."

▪Kitty Cat and Mouse▪

That, seemingly, remained in the future. For the time being, the couple "refused to change their lives just because they were Mr. and Mrs. JFK Jr.," says Carolyn's friend Wilmot. "She'd jog and he'd play Frisbee and they'd both walk the dog." They continued to Rollerblade and kayak. When they worked out together at the Cape Cod Athletic Club in Hyannis, says Joe Duran, the club's assistant manager, "They'd smile and give each other little glimpses across the room."

Family and friends regarded them as soulmates who shared both an easy sophistication and an appealing lack of pretension. He called her "Kitty Cat"; she called him "Mouse." He looked forward to coming home at day's end. "She was very much Mrs. John Kennedy in an old-fashioned way," says Wilmot. "He didn't want a wife that went to the office. He liked the fact she was there when he came home." Evenings, they cooked in or shared quiet dinners with friends.

Gradually Bessette seemed to get a grip on how to handle the pesky press. In May of this year she told the New York *Daily News* that she'd stopped reading about herself in the papers and was "a happy person, and maybe a better person, for not knowing." She learned from her husband. "She admired the way he lived in a fishbowl and remained normal," says Wilmot.

The weekend before the crash, the couple stopped by the scruffy Lamppost bar on Martha's Vineyard for a round of margaritas with friends. When it came time to settle up, the friends grabbed the bill. As they prepared to exit, Bessette discreetly approached their waitress, Meredith Katz, 20, a student at Tulane University. "Did they tip you enough?" Carolyn asked. With that, she pressed another $15 or $20 on Katz, saying, "I know how expensive rents are here on the island."

Through it all, the spark that had drawn Bessette and Kennedy to each other burned bright. One evening at Chez Josephine, a French restaurant in Manhattan's Broadway theater district, Kennedy asked piano player Chris Curtis to play a special Elton John song for Bessette. It was the one whose lyrics conclude,

I hope you don't mind
that I put down in words
how wonderful life is
with you in the world.

12

FINAL FLIGHT

In New York City, the second week of the seventh month of the last year of the millennium dawned blistering hot and brightly promising for John Kennedy. On Monday, July 12, still hobbled by the cast on his left ankle from the Memorial Day landing mishap in his Buckeye, Kennedy copiloted his Piper Saratoga II with a flight instructor to Markham, Ontario, to meet with a potential investor who might shore up *George.*

Five hours later, as he prepared to fly home, he chatted with Keith Stein, the Toronto businessman who had brokered the meeting, about his love of flying, his magazine, his wife. "He asked me how old I was, and I asked him how old he was," says Stein, 35. "We were talking about how quickly time flies. And fate. He said, 'If you can't control it, there's no point worrying about it.'"

Returning to the glamorous bustle of his life, Kennedy on Tuesday evening dropped by a British ad agency party in downtown Manhat-

On Saturday, July 17, the day after Kennedy's plane failed to reach Martha's Vineyard, mourning fans erected a spontaneous shrine outside John and Carolyn's apartment in lower Manhattan.

tan for a trendy new magazine. Wednesday he attended a meeting involving Reaching Up, the charity he had established in 1987 to support efforts on behalf of the disabled. Thursday morning a doctor at Lenox Hill Hospital removed the cast from his ankle and, he told friends, cleared him for solo flight again. That night he took in a Yankees-Braves game from the field-level box of Yanks owner George Steinbrenner.

Friday morning, July 16, Kennedy discussed *George's* prospects with Jack Kliger, the recently named president of Hachette-Filipacchi. He left the discussion feeling "fairly positive," according to Kliger. After meetings with *George* staffers that afternoon JFK began to focus on the weekend ahead: the marriage of his cousin Rory Kennedy, 30, a documentary filmmaker, to Mark Bailey, 30, a writer who also works in film. He placed his daily call to his sister Caroline, sent a consoling e-mail to a friend whose mother had recently died, then caught a workout at the gym. Carolyn, meanwhile, dashed to Saks Fifth Avenue in midtown to buy a dress—a $1,640 black silk crepe Alber Elbaz, a designer working for Yves Saint Laurent—for the wedding.

Kennedy was met at his office at 6:30 by Lauren, one of Carolyn's twin sisters. A respected investment banker and a vice-president at Morgan Stanley Dean Witter, Lauren, 34, had asked to hitch a ride with the Kennedys to Martha's Vineyard before they proceeded on to Hyannis Port. Together, John and Lauren set out for Essex airport in Fairfield, New Jersey, in Kennedy's white Hyundai convertible. The weekend getaway traffic was snarled through the Lincoln Tunnel, so that it was after 8 p.m. when they finally pulled into the gas station across from the airfield where Kennedy often purchased last-minute, pre-flight supplies. On this night, he bought three bananas, mineral water and some AA batteries.

■CLEARED FOR TAKEOFF■

While Kennedy was preparing the Piper for takeoff, Carolyn arrived from Manhattan by car service. At 8:38, just after sunset, the three took off from runway 22, with Kennedy at the controls and the Bessette sisters in the rear. Hugging the Connecticut coastline, Kennedy climbed to 5,600 feet, then began the 40-mile passage across ocean waters.

Kyle Bailey, a local pilot at Essex airport, told reporters that he'd been surprised by Kennedy's decision to fly. Bailey had canceled his own plans to fly to the Vineyard earlier Friday evening because of a haze that was obscuring from view a nearby mountain ridge—a vision test, he said, "that most pilots use at the airport."

The Essex tower, however, had cleared Kennedy for takeoff. Subsequent reports indicated that information provided by the Federal Aviation Administration and the Weather Bureau may have erroneously described visibility at Kennedy's destination as more than eight miles—safely above the three-mile minimum required for a pilot navigating, as Kennedy did, largely by naked eye, under so-called visual flight rules, or VFR.

Dark as a Shut Closet

The best description of what Kennedy probably encountered as he approached Martha's Vineyard was provided by Dr. Bob Arnot, chief medical correspondent for NBC, who had flown his own private plane past the island less than a half hour earlier. "When I looked down at Martha's Vineyard, I could not see it. I saw nothing," he says. "It's as if somebody put you in a closet and shut the door." In order to land, Arnot had switched to instrument flight rules, or IFR—relying solely on the gauges on his control panel. "I haven't been in conditions like that for years," he said. "I have 5,000 hours and I had a problem."

Kennedy, by contrast, had logged only 300 hours aloft, and was authorized to pilot only under VFR. He'd logged perhaps just half of the roughly 50 hours of flight time needed to achieve his instrument rating. The consensus of aviation experts is that when the horizon disappears in darkness or bad weather the body's sense of speed and direction can prove misleading—and deadly. Kennedy may indeed have consulted his instruments, but without proven

As Ethel Kennedy (center) and other family members waited anxiously for news over the weekend, federal agencies and officials from five states mounted a massive, round-the-clock search for the missing bodies.

expertise in navigating by them he may have become disoriented.

At 9:15, about 34 miles from the island, Kennedy began a slow descent to 2,300 feet, perhaps attempting to drop beneath the obscuring haze. At 9:39, some 18 miles from the Martha's Vineyard airport, the Piper began to turn to the right—away from the airport—and climbed from 2,300 feet to 2,600 feet. Then it began losing altitude sharply and gaining speed. Apparently corkscrewing down at a rate 10 times normal speed, it dropped 400 feet in less than a minute and a half, then another 600 feet in just nine seconds.

A novice pilot's instinct in this kind of steep turn is to pull the control yoke back to lift the nose. But unless the pilot first levels the wings—something very difficult to do in those conditions except by instruments—the maneuver only tightens the dive into what pilots call a "dead man's spiral." Whatever the cause, the final horrific plunge lasted only about 30 to 40 seconds. Impact with the ocean's surface ripped the plane to pieces and killed all three occupants instantly.

▪ THE VIGIL ▪

Meanwhile, in Hyannis Port on Cape Cod, Rory's rehearsal dinner was underway at the Kennedy compound. It was a magical evening for the youngest of Ethel and Bobby's 11 children, "full of joy and happiness," said one guest. "They [had] made a quilt for Rory and Mark," said a family friend. "Everyone made a square with a footprint or handprint or something representing them."

Under the many-peaked white tent near the water's edge, the 100 dinner guests were unaware of the drama unfolding 20 miles to the southwest at the tiny airport on Martha's Vineyard where two friends of Lauren Bessette's had been waiting to pick her up since 8:30. After the concerned friends reported the delay to Adam Budd, 21, an airport intern, he phoned the Federal Aviation Administration at 10:05 and asked if Kennedy's plane could be traced. Budd, who did not made it clear the plane was overdue, was informed that the FAA did not give out such information over the phone. At 2:15 a.m. Saturday, July 17, more than five hours after Kennedy's anticipated arrival, a Kennedy family friend phoned the Coast Guard. Only then was a search launched.

At 7 a.m., President Clinton was notified that Kennedy's plane

■ *On July 20, four days after the crash, Massachussetts State Police divers from the Underwater Recovery Unit entered waters west of Martha's Vineyard. The bodies would be discovered the next day.*

was missing. "Let's make sure we're doing everything we can to find them," he responded. As the Civil Air Patrol, Coast Guard and Air National Guard hunted from the skies, Coast Guard cutters, patrol boats and search-and-rescue ships trawled the 190 nautical miles stretching between Long Island and Cape Cod. By noon Saturday, the Central Intelligence Agency had been enlisted to lend three of its advanced tracking satellites to the effort.

At the Kennedy compound, around 8:30 a.m., family members began alerting the 275 guests by telephone that the wedding, scheduled for 6 p.m., would be postponed indefinitely. The morning dragged on. Some 50 friends and family gathered on Ethel Kennedy's porch for an impromptu Mass.

All too versed in tragedy, the Kennedys, huddling around TVs and radios, tried to keep each other's spirits up. "They were saying, 'There's still hope. Never say never,'" says a family friend.

Meanwhile, on vacation in Stanley, Idaho, Caroline and her family had settled into suite 231 of the Mountain Village Resort on Friday night. The plan was to celebrate both her husband Edwin Schlossberg's 54th birthday and the couple's 13th anniversary on July 19 by rafting with their three children through the 2.3-million-acre wilderness known as the River of No Return. By 7 p.m., Saturday, the trip was canceled. The family, in shock, headed back to New York aboard a private plane.

Down the coast in Greenwich, Conn., Carolyn's family had been notified at 5 a.m. A friend of her mother, Ann Freeman, said, "Ann was hopeful for a while. And then common sense prevailed."

▪EVIDENCE IN THE TIDES▪

By mid-afternoon Saturday, the search was narrowed to a 20-by-20-mile area off the Vineyard. Bits of airplane carpeting, a landing wheel and a headrest had already washed ashore, but the first personal clue to be pulled from the waters was a piece of black luggage with a business card in a clear pocket that read "Lauren G. Bessette." Damon

■ *On July 21, Ted Kennedy, who had witnessed the retrieval of his nephew's body from 116 feet of water, stood by as a group of Kennedy cousins helped load the remains of a victim into a van.*

Seligson, the Boston lawyer who retrieved the bag from the waves, recalls, "I had a gut-wrenching feeling. It's haunting, really haunting."

Chillingly, this evidence was soon joined by a black cosmetics bag containing a prescription bottle labeled "Carolyn Kennedy." Late Sunday night, with no bodies found, the Coast Guard announced it was switching its mission from "search and rescue to search and recover." The flag at the Kennedy compound was lowered to half-mast.

As the recovery operation extended through Tuesday, then into Wednesday, President Clinton defended the extraordinary scope and expense, rarely undertaken for the wreck of a private plane. "Because of the role of the Kennedy family in our national lives and because of the enormous losses they have sustained in our lifetimes, I thought it was appropriate," he said.

Early on Wednesday, July 21, word finally came that the three bodies had been found, still strapped into their seats, upside down in 116 feet of water a few miles off Gay Head, where Kennedy had frolicked as a boy. Shortly after noon, Ted Kennedy, accompanied by his two

sons, Representative Patrick Kennedy of Rhode Island and Edward, was taken to the Navy salvage ship *Grasp*, so they could be present when the remains were hauled up from the deep.

On July 30, the National Transportation Safety Board, which had put out word that its investigation would continue for at least another six months, announced that the wreckage showed no sign of in-flight breakup or fire.

▪ CAROLINE'S WAY ▪

During the search, Caroline and her family waited for word at their country house in Bridgehampton, N.Y., on Long Island. Caroline in recent years had put a distance between herself and the Kennedy clan she considered too often raucous and reckless. But at least one friend maintains, "She wanted to go to Hyannis Port, but everyone said it was a [media] zoo and advised her to go to New York instead."

On Sunday, the 18th, she was joined by Ted Kennedy, who offered solace and distraction, shooting baskets with her three children. Caroline was also visited by some of her favorite cousins, among them NBC correspondent Maria Shriver, who had served as matron of honor at her wedding, as she had at Shriver's.

There was the prospect of a funeral to discuss—no small matter for a family who through the decades had instructed the nation in the art of dignified memorial services. One version has it that Uncle Ted deferred to Caroline from the start. A Kennedy cousin, however, told the London *Daily Mail* that the Senator was trying to get special dispensation for John to be buried next to his parents in the military's Arlington National Cemetery. By this account, when Caroline learned of the plan, she summoned her uncle to Long Island. "She told him there was to be no public ceremony," said the cousin.

In consultation with the Bessette family, it was decided that all three victims' remains would be cremated and the ashes scattered at sea—a farewell ensuring utmost family privacy and no gravesite to attract generations of the curious. Kennedy had let it be known that he wished to be buried at sea. Former White House social secretary Letitia Baldrige noted, "Something quiet and elegant, like Jackie would have done it." Burial at sea befit the son of President Kennedy, who in 1962 memorably commented: "We are tied to the ocean. And when we go back to the sea ... we are going back from whence we came."

On Thursday morning, July 22, 17 relatives were taken by the cutter *Sanibel* to the Navy destroyer *Briscoe*. Beyond range of cameras, the Kennedy and Bessette families spread the ashes off the *Briscoe's* stern. As the ship steamed back into port the mourners released into the wind a flurry of flower petals, believed to have been plucked from the 7,000 blossoms originally intended as decoration for Rory's wedding reception. (Rory, for her part, would slip off to Greece with Bailey and marry on August 2. Attended by only 25 guests, the wedding at the picture-perfect villa of shipping tycoon Vardis Vardinoyannis was reportedly the sort of low-key affair the couple had wanted all along.)

The next day, in a memorial service also orchestrated by Caroline, 315 family members, friends and notables—among them the Clin-

As 17 members of the Kennedy and Bessette families stood on the stern of the Navy destroyer Briscoe, *the ashes of the three victims were scattered over the waters near Martha's Vineyard.*

ton family and boxing great Muhammad Ali, a hero of JFK Jr.'s—gathered in uptown Manhattan at St. Thomas More Catholic Church, where Jackie Kennedy Onasssis and her children had once worshipped. Ted Kennedy and his sister Eunice had hoped the service would be held at the much larger St. Patrick's Cathedral. "But St. Patrick's reminded Caroline too much of Bobby Kennedy's funeral," says a friend. "The family totally respected that she wanted it in a small church."

▪EVERY GIFT BUT LENGTH OF YEARS▪

His voice breaking, Ted eulogized his nephew. All too much like his ill-fated father, Ted somberly noted, John "had every gift but length of years." Caroline, who'd asked her uncle to deliver the eulogy, hugged him as he descended the pulpit, and then offered her own brief tribute. Quoting from Shakespeare's play *The Tempest*, in which her brother had appeared at Brown in 1981, she said, "We are such stuff as dreams are made on, and our little life is rounded with a sleep."

"Cool and composed," Caroline, according to one guest, gave no hint how she felt about the 1,000 onlookers crowding the sidewalks, just as she would later give no sign how she felt about the many memorial services that non-family members would hold in cities around the country. But after getting into a black limousine, she broke through her usual reserve and acknowledged the well-wishers by lowering her window and waving.

The tragic drama that for a full week had gripped the hearts and minds of people around the world swiftly drew to a close. As floral tributes continued to amass outside John and Carolyn's New York City apartment building and pour into Hyannis Port, the Kennedys asked that future arrangements be sent to hospitals, or that donations be made to Kennedy's favorite charities. Only with his passing were Kennedy's friends learning of all the charitable organizations that had benefited from his energy and patronage.

That, perhaps, was the most telling statement of all about the handsome, charming man who wore his fame and his family name so lightly. Once asked what he found most intriguing about his famous father, Kennedy had offered a simple tribute: "I think the most interesting thing about him is that you realize that he was just a man, that he lived a life, like anybody else." In projecting that kind of unassuming ease in honoring his legacy while living fully a life of his own, John F. Kennedy Jr. enjoyed his greatest success and secured his place in America's heart.

▪ Timeline ▪

1960   Born November 25th in Washington, D.C., seventeen days after his father was elected the 35th President of the United States.

1963   President Kennedy assassinated in Dallas. Three days later, on his third birthday, John, Jr. salutes his father's flag-draped casket during the state funeral.

1965   Enrolls at St. David's School in Manhattan, a private Catholic institution for boys.

1968   Bobby Kennedy assassinated in Los Angeles after winning the California Democratic primary.

1968   Jacqueline Kennedy marries Greek shipping magnate Aristotle Onassis.

1979   Graduates from Phillips Academy in Andover, Mass. Enrolls at Brown University.

1983   Graduates from Brown with a degree in history.

1984   Takes a position with the New York City Office of Business Development.

1988   Introduces his uncle, Senator Edward Kennedy, in a rousing speech at the Democratic National Convention in Atlanta.

1988   PEOPLE names him "The Sexiest Man Alive."

1989   Graduates from New York University Law School, and begins work as a prosecutor in the Manhattan district attorney's office.

1990   After two unsuccessful attempts, passes the bar exam.

1993   Resigns from district attorney's office with a perfect 6–0 conviction record.

1994   Jacqueline Kennedy Onassis dies of cancer.

1994   Ends five-and-a-half year relationship with actress Daryl Hannah.

1996   Launches *George*, a bipartisan political and popular culture magazine.

■ TIMELINE ■

1996   Marries Carolyn Bessette, a publicist for Calvin Klein, on September 21. Only 40 attend the secret ceremony on an island off the coast of Georgia.

1998   Receives his pilot's license.

1999   Dies on July 16 with his wife and his sister-in-law, Lauren Bessette, when the plane he is piloting crashes into the sea near Martha's Vineyard.

▪ NOTE ▪

Over the years, PEOPLE reporters have
interviewed many of those close to John F. Kennedy Jr.
personally and professionally. These interviews have
been drawn upon throughout this book.

▪ AUTHOR INTERVIEWS ▪

Don Armstrong
Hugh Auchincloss Jr.
Jamie Auchincloss
Ethan Bagg
Letitia Baldrige
William Benson
Roy Black
Owen Carragher
Oleg Cassini
Ralph Diaz
Joe Duran
Smith Galtney
Barbara Gibson
Vishv Bandhu Gupta
Christina Haag
Nigel Hamilton
A. E. Hotchner
Lloyd Howard

Charlie King
Laurence Leamer
Wendy Leigh
Jacques Lowe
Richard Lowe
Frank Mankiewicz
Bob Mann
Kiki Moutsatsos
Meredith Price
Elen Rothenberg
Pierre Salinger
Rajeev Sethi
Hilary Shepard-Turner
Hugh Sidey
Jonathan Soroff
Keith Stein
Ken Sunshine
Jack Valenti

▪ ADDITIONAL SOURCES ▪

Carl Sferrazza Anthony, *As We Remember Her,*
HarperCollins, N.Y., 1997
C. David Heymann, *A Woman Named Jackie,*
Lyle Stuart, N.Y., 1989
Current Biography, 1996, The H. W.
Wilson Compnay, N.Y. 1996
Christopher Andersen, *Jackie After Jack:
Portrait of the Lady,* Warner Books, 1998
John H. Davis, *Jacqueline Bouvier: An*

Intimate Memoir, John Wiley & Sons, Inc.,
N.Y., 1996
Nigel Hamilton, *JFK: Reckless Youth,*
Random House, N.Y., 1992
Stephen Spignesi, *The J.F.K. Jr Scrapbook,*
Citadel Press, Carol Publishing Group,
N. J., 1997
Edward Klein, *Just Jackie: Her Private
Years,* Balantine Books, N.Y., 1998

◾ Sources (cont.) ◾

Caroline Latham & Jeannie Sakol, *The Kennedy Encyclopedia,* New American Library, N.Y., 1989

Peter Collier & David Horowitz, *The Kennedys: An American Drama,* Summit Books, N. Y., 1984

Laurence Leamer, *The Kennedy Women: The Saga of an American Family,* Villard Books, N.Y. 1994

Wendy Leigh, *Prince Charming: The John F. Kennedy, Jr., Story,* A Signet Book, 1993

Jay David Andrews, *Young Kennedys: The New Generation,* Avon Books, N. Y. 1998

John Diamond, Associated Press, April 7, 1988

Associated Press, May 24, 1994

Adrian Walker, *Boston Globe,* August 12, 1997

Steven Brill, *Brill's Content,* March, 1999

Business Week, October 30, 1995

Cynthia Hanson, *Chicago Magazine,* October 1993

Daniel Jeffreys, *Daily Mail,* July 24, 1999

Keith J. Kelly, *Daily News,* July 27, 1997

Michael Daly, *Daily News,* July 21, 1999

Mitchell Fink, Emily Gest, *Daily News,* July 21, 1999

Lewis H. Lapham, *Harper's Magazine,* November, 1995

Larry King Live, September 28, 1995

Brad Darrach, *Life,* March, 1995

Life Special Edition 1999

Anthony Wilson-Smith, *Maclean's,* July 26, 1999

Dennis Duggan, *Newsday,* November 29, 1988

Newsday, September 9, 1993

Pat Wechsler, *Newsday,* November 24, 1993

Shain/Scaduto, *Newsday,* May 24, 1994

Evan Thomas, *Newsweek,* May 30, 1994

Newsweek, August 14, 1994

Marth Brant, Evan Thomas, *Newsweek,* August 14, 1995

Kenneth Auchincloss, *Newsweek,* July 26, 1999

Barbara Kantrowitz, *Newsweek, JFK Jr. : His Life and the Kennedy Legacy, A Memorial Edition*

Rebecca Mead, *New York,* August 7, 1995

Rebecca Mead, *New York,* October 7, 1996

New York, August 2, 1999

Robert J. Donovan, *New York Herald Tribune,* November 26, 1960

Bill Hoffmann, *New York Post,* August 3, 1999

Palm Beach Post, July 18, 1999

Sacramento Bee, October 15, 1995

Michael Gross, *St. Louis Post-Dispatch,* April 12, 1989

The Boston Globe, April 14, 1994

Meg Vaillancourt, *The Boston Globe,* August 14, 1994

Rick Moody, *The New Yorker,* August 2, 1999

The New York Times, September 10, 1974

The New York Times, March 2, 1982

The New York Times, July 26, 1992

Robert McFadden, *The New York Times,* May 20, 1994

Deirdre Carmody, *The New York Times,* September 8, 1995

Elizabeth Bumiller, *The New York Times,* July 29, 1996

The New York Times, July 18, 1999

The New York Times, July 22, 1999

Alex Kuczynski, *The New York Times,* July 22, 1999

Mike Allen, *The New York Times,* July 22, 1999

The New York Times, July 23, 1999

The New York Times, July 24, 1999

Joyce Walder, John Kennedy, *The Washington Post,* December 17, 1981

The Washington Post, December 25, 1981

Ann L. Trebbe, *The Washington Post,* March 25, 1982

Mary Jordan, *The Washington Post,* November 19, 1991

Ann Gerhart, *The Washington Post,* October 9, 1996

Time, May 27, 1974

Martha Duffy, *Time,* May 30, 1994

Bruce Handy, *Time,* July 18, 1995

James Collins, *Time,* October 7, 1996

Arthur Schlesinger, Jr., *Time,* July 26, 1999

Richard Lacayo, *Time,* July 26, 1999

Eric Pooley, *Time,* July 26, 1999

John Cloud, *Time,* August 2, 1999

Jeffrey Kluger, Mark Thompson, *Time,* August 2, 1999

Margaret Carlson, *Time,* August 2, 1999

Today (NBC News Transcripts), July 19, 1999

Carole Agues, *Toronto Star,* September 12, 1993

USA Today, March 31, 1994

Katy Kelly, *USA Today,* May 18, 1998

Alan Levin, Kevin Johnson, Deborah Sharp, *USA Today,* July 22, 1999

▪ PHOTOGRAPHY CREDITS ▪

▪ ABOUT THE AUTHORS ▪

J.D. Reed is the author of three books of poetry and one and a half novels (he co-authored a mystery with his wife). A former staff writer at SPORTS ILLUSTRATED and TIME, he is an Associate Editor of PEOPLE Magazine.

Kyle Smith, a staff writer at PEOPLE since 1996, is a former reporter for the New York bureau of the Associated Press and *The New York Post.* He has also written for *The Times* of London, *New York* magazine and *The New York Times Magazine.* He lives in New York City.

Jill Smolowe, author of *An Empty Lap: One Couple's Journey to Parenthood,* has been on the writing staffs of *Newsweek* and TIME. She is an Associate Editor of PEOPLE.